INSIGHT POCKET GUIDE

FLORIDA

Discovery
CHANNEL

APA PUBLICATIONS
Part of the Langenscheidt Publishing Group

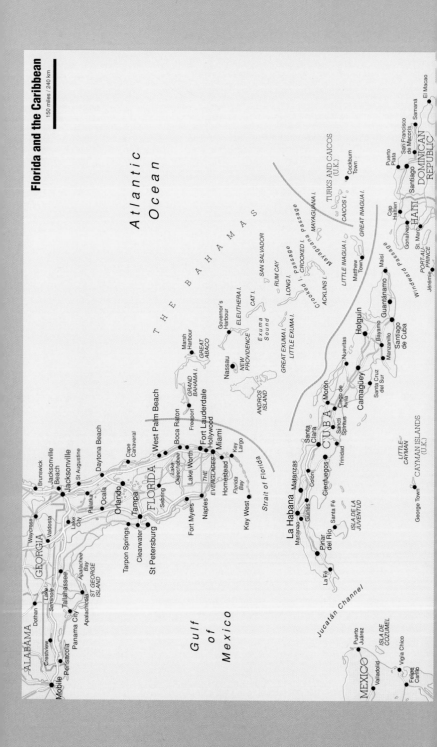

Florida and the Caribbean

150 miles / 240 km

Welcome!

This guidebook combines the interests and enthusiasms of two of the world's best-known information providers: Insight Guides, who have set the standard for visual travel guides since 1970, and Discovery Channel, the world's premier source of non-fiction television programming.

Its aim is to help you make the most of your stay in the land of magic kingdoms, offbeat islands, honky-tonk beach towns, Cuban exiles, sun-tanned surfers, Native Americans, ocean breezes, plastic flamingoes, orange perfume. Welcome to Florida.

In this guidebook Joann Biondi, Insight Guides' correspondent in Miami, helps visitors discover the best of Florida during a short stay with a series of itineraries based on four key areas: Orlando, Tampa/St Petersburg, Miami and Key West, beginning in the center of the state, then heading west and then southeast and south. Supporting the itineraries are sections on history and culture, eating out, nightlife and a calendar of special events, plus a fact-packed practical information section.

 Joann Biondi has lived and worked as a journalist in Florida since 1974. She says there is no place in the world she would rather live. 'I like hearing the wild parrots that squawk each morning, going for a swim on New Year's Eve, and picking fresh oranges from the tree in my yard. I've had northerners ask, "How can you live there," and others say, "I wish I were you." It is a place that makes you realize that making a life is more important than making a living.' With the help of this guide, she hopes that some of her love of Florida will rub off on you.

C O N T E N T S

Pages 2/3:
Miami's
famous beach

Miami

Key West

Pages 8/9: the Scorpion ride at Busch Gardens

HISTORY &

The modern-day tourists, positioning their beach towels so that they get their fair share of Florida sunshine, are just the end of a long line of pilgrims who believe that they too are entitled to a small slice of the state. For centuries, Florida has been a magnet that has attracted conquerors, settlers, developers, dreamers, escapees, refugees, immigrants and travelers. It is a place where people come for rest, rejuvenation, retirement. And to start anew.

Early History

In the beginning there were Native Americans. Timucuans, Calusas, Apalachees, Tequestas, Mayaimas, Apalachicolas, Miccosukees, and Seminoles. But, as in most parts of the Americas, the Indian tribes were no match for the European settlers who came to conquer the land and the peoples they had found. Juan Ponce de Leon, sailing under the Spanish flag, was the first explorer credited with 'discovering' Florida in 1513. Continuing the Spanish conquest, de Leon was followed by Panfilo de Narvaez and Hernando de Soto who both sailed into Tampa Bay. Then came another Spaniard, Pedro Menendez de Aviles, who in 1565 founded St Augustine, the oldest city in the US. For a brief period in the mid-1500s, there was a small French settlement near St Augustine, but it was quickly destroyed by the Spaniards who detested the 'French pirates'. In

Chief Satouriona befriended French settlers

Culture

Hernando de Soto

the 300 years that followed, the Spanish and the British vied for control of the Florida peninsula.

By the 1800s, Florida was a haven for runaway slaves fleeing the South and in 1821 the United States gained control of the peninsula. Americans began staking their claims to land along the banks of the Miami river.

The mid-1800s were marked by a series of violent and bloody Seminole Indian Wars, as the tribes tried to resist what the white settlers called progress. About 1,500 slaves joined the Seminole tribe and fought alongside the Native Americans against the white settlers. One of the most noted confrontations was the Dade Massacre in which Major Francis L Dade (after whom Miami's county was named) was killed.

When Florida became a state in 1845, the population, including 39,000 black slaves, was 87,000. During the American Civil War, Florida sided with the Confederate South. It mustered its minuscule population and its even smaller budget to wage war. Its participation was brief and limited, but devastating.

By the time the war was over, much of developed Florida lay in ruins, destroyed by the Union troops. However, in the 1860s and '70s, the first of the northern developers, whose names are now immortalized in local street signs, had arrived in the state and were beginning to claim their stake in Miami. Florida was already on the road to recovery.

Henry M Flagler

The Boom Begins

Toward the end of the 1800s, Florida experienced a substantial increase in population growth and development – by 1880, the state's population had soared to 270,000. In 1885, the American Medical Association endorsed the St Petersburg area as the healthiest place in the US, and the land boom that would stretch into the 1920s began.

Two industrious railroad tycoons, both named Henry, were responsible for most of Florida's early growth. Henry M Flagler, a retired northern oil baron, decided that Florida was not only up for grabs, but was his for the taking. Flagler built a series of palatial hotels and even created his own railroad – the Florida East Coast Railroad – to deliver tourists to his doors. He started his first Florida hotel in St Augustine in 1885, and by 1896 had extended his resort building and railroad tracks to Miami. In 1912 his train roared into Key West. At about the same time Henry B Plant was busy developing Florida's west coast. Plant built the Atlantic Coastline Railroad that linked Richmond, Virginia, with Tampa, and then constructed the luxurious Tampa Bay Hotel to lure tourists.

The early 1900s brought more growth. Architect Addison Mizner built a playground for the richest of the rich in Palm Beach, millionaire Carl Fisher turned what was nothing more than a barren

Railroad barons paved the way for economic expansion

sandbar into the resort paradise known as Miami Beach, and George Merrick created the beautiful Mediterranean-style city of Coral Gables near Miami. Things in Florida, at least in South Florida, were looking great until two hurricanes, one in 1926 and the other in 1928, wreaked havoc on the southern part of the state. And then the stock market crash and the Great Depression of 1929 added more misery to the state's economy.

Tourism Takes Hold

By the start of World War II, 2½ million tourists a year were visiting Florida, and the state's population had reached 2 million. Following the war, more and more tourists began to head south for a much-needed Florida vacation. Throughout the 1940s, '50s and '60s, hundreds of small motels and quirky roadside attractions sprung up across the state. Families from all over America made the slow drive down the highway to Florida, stopping for sips of fresh orange juice along the way. They visited alligator zoos,

A 1954 postcard depicting Palm Beach

pineapple farms, and broad, empty beaches. In its early years, Florida's tourism industry, although already seen as a golden egg, was simple, wholesome and authentic.

Along with tourism, the 1940s, '50s and '60s meant the growth of another Florida industry – space exploration. Chosen for the purpose because of its year-round good weather and offshore buffer zone should something go wrong, Cape Canaveral began launching missiles into space in the late 1940s. In an attempt to keep up with the Soviet Union's space explorations, the US government poured billions of dollars into its Florida-based space program and launched its first satellite, *Explorer I*, in 1958. It was from Cape Canaveral (now called the Kennedy Space Center) that astronaut Neil Armstrong blasted off for the moon in 1969. The space program, a tourist attraction in itself, provides many jobs and is an economic boost for the state.

Although tourism is Florida's main source of revenue, the agriculture and cattle industries, as well as international banking, are prominent economic factors. About two-thirds of the nation's citrus fruits – oranges, grapefruits, lemons, limes and tangerines – come

13

Off to work they go: Mickey and the seven construction workers

from Florida. The vast orange groves of central Florida alone produce about 250 million crates of oranges and 800 million gallons of orange juice a year. So a rare Florida cold spell in winter not only worries the tourism promoters, but farmers too.

Enter Mickey Mouse

One of the more dramatic changes in modern Florida history occurred in 1971, the year that Mickey Mouse came to town. The opening of Walt Disney World south of Orlando forever altered the atmosphere of Florida and transformed its tourism industry from a small-scale, mom-and-pop business into a multi-national, mass-market giant like no other in the world. Along with Mickey Mouse came more and more enormous hotels, fast-food restaurants, super-highways, expanded airports, and junky souvenir shops selling glittery mouse ears. Following in Disney's path came a new genre of tourist attraction in Florida: self-contained, expensive theme parks of fantasyland fun.

More New Faces

Along with Mickey Mouse, lots of other new faces have made their way to Florida during the past few decades, turning it into the fourth largest state in terms of population in the US (almost 15 million). The in-migration of American retirees, which started over 50 years ago, is never-ending. After spending a lifetime working hard in the Northeast or Midwest, many senior citizens feel that retirement in Florida is their due reward in the last leg of the American dream. The state's elderly population continues to rise and retirement communities and condominiums have sprouted up to meet their needs. Snowbirds, people who come for the winter, are another Florida phenomenon. Once predominantly American, the snowbirds of recent years include wealthy people from around the world and celebrities who take pride in owning a vacation home in Florida.

Following the Cuban Revolution in 1959, Cuban refugees fleeing the Communist takeover of their island began streaming into the state. In the past 30 years, over 1 million Cubans have left their homeland — many of them via small, rubber rafts — and settled down to start new lives in Florida. Their presence, especially in South Florida, has pumped young blood and enthusiasm into the economy, and drastically changed the ethnic make-up of the state.

In addition to the Cuban immigrants, hundreds of thousands of Nicaraguans, Guatemalans, Venezuelans, and Colombians have also migrated to Florida, swelling the Latin American population to such a degree that in some areas Spanish is spoken more than English. Florida has also received a large number of West Indian immigrants in the past 20 years, including Jamaicans, Haitians, and Bahamians who have added even more multi-cultural spice to the state's rich ethnic stew.

Old-fashioned Florida Crackers, descendants of early white settlers, are an endangered species, but can still be found throughout the central and northern parts of the state. What's left of the Seminole and Miccosukee Indian populations in Florida tend to live on self-contained reservations scattered throughout the state. Many of

Haitian family gathering

the reservations have been turned into money-making tourist attractions where they now sell arts and crafts. Some of the Indian reservations, immune to laws that regulate gambling in the rest of the state, now offer bingo games as another way of generating income.

15

Sweeping Changes

The city of Orlando has enjoyed unprecedented growth, due in large part to Disney World and its theme park neighbors. The arrivals are not merely tourists – in the past 10 years the population of the three counties that straddle Orlando has swelled by 102 people *per day*. The area created more factory jobs than any other place in the United States, and employment rose by almost 150 percent. Major industries followed suit, with the American Automobile Association, AT&T, and Westinghouse setting up shop within a few years of each other.

In the wake of Hurricane Andrew

The most recent visitor to land on Florida's shores was a brutal storm named Andrew. In August 1992 a category 5 hurricane, packing 160-mph winds and a 12-ft tidal surge, slammed into South Florida. During his four-hour visit, Hurricane Andrew destroyed over 60,000 homes and left 150,000 people homeless. The worst natural disaster ever to hit the US, Andrew left a 25-mile wide path of destruction estimated at $30 billion. Hardest hit were the rural areas of Homestead, Florida City and Kendall about 20 miles south of downtown Miami. Fortunately for the area's tourism industry, most of Miami's main attractions suffered only minimal damage. Although the rebuilding of the devastated areas is expected to take decades – and was not helped by more severe weather and flooding in March 1993 – the entire state of Florida has pitched in to help their neighbors to the south.

This willingness to help out is indicative of the pioneer spirit of Floridians. The heady mix of endless sunshine, good beaches, Art Deco, and amusements galore, means that the state of Florida will continue to attract pioneers for the foreseeable future.

The fun goes on

Historical Highlights

5000BC An unknown, aboriginal culture inhabits the northern part of the Florida peninsula, surviving by fishing, hunting and agriculture.

AD300–1000 Highly developed Native American tribes inhabit many parts of the peninsula.

1498 Map-maker John Cabot, sailing on the behalf of the British, creates a crude map of Florida.

1513 Spanish explorer Juan Ponce de Leon 'discovers' Florida while searching for the island of Bimini.

1521 De Leon returns with 200 settlers.

1565 St Augustine, the oldest city in the US, is founded by Pedro Menendez de Aviles of Spain.

1763–83 The British accept Florida from Spain in exchange for Havana; following the Revolutionary War, Britain trades Florida back to Spain.

1821 The US gains control of Florida from Spain and hundreds of runaway slaves from the north settle in Florida.

mid-1800s A series of Seminole Wars erupts as Native American tribes try to hold on to their land.

1845 Florida becomes a US state.

1861 As a major slave-holding state, Florida secedes from the Union and joins the southern Confederacy in preparation for the American Civil War.

1865 The Civil War ends, costing Florida $20 million in damages and over 5,000 lives.

1885 A wave of Cuban cigar makers settles in Tampa.

1896 Henry M Flagler's Florida East Coast Railroad makes its way from St Augustine to Miami. And in 1912, continues on to Key West.

1915 Miami Beach becomes a city, as casinos and cafés blossom.

1920s A so-called land-boom envelops the state; houses and hotels are built throughout Florida.

1928 A massive hurricane leaves over 2,000 people dead near Lake Okeechobee.

1930s Miami Beach's Art Deco hotels are built and tourism begins to thrive in South Florida.

1947 Cape Canaveral launches its first series of missiles into space.

1950s Post-World War II travelers start to flock to Florida and large-scale tourism begins.

1959 Fidel Castro takes control of Cuba and triggers a massive influx of Cuban refugees to Florida.

1964 The US Civil Rights Act is passed. Blacks in Florida begin to overcome severe racial discrimination and segregation.

1970s US economic recession badly hurts Florida. President Nixon vacations on Key Biscayne as four Miamians instigate the Watergate political scandal. Conditions in the Caribbean island of Haiti worsen and thousands of Haitians sail rickety boats to Miami.

1971 Walt Disney World opens near Orlando.

1984 The glitzy television series *Miami Vice* premiers, vastly changing the public image of Florida.

1992–3 Hurricane Andrew blasts South Florida, leaving 150,000 people homeless; then a 'no name' storm spawns 50 tornados which kill 51 people across the state.

1995 Governor Lawton Chiles files a $1.2 billion lawsuit against the Tobacco Institute for the state's costs in treating Medicare smokers.

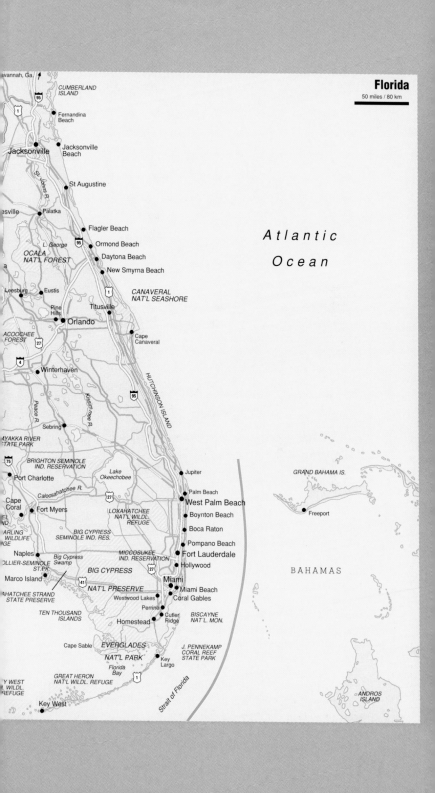

Day itine

The state of Florida encompasses a much larger area than most tourists imagine. The following tour selections therefore assume that you will be traveling through the state by car. If you are staying in Florida for only one week, it is unlikely that you'll be able to take in all the areas highlighted in this book. You might have to concentrate on just two or three destinations. However, you have in your hands a complete listing of the more well-known attractions as well as a fair sprinkling of offbeat places that are often overlooked by travelers.

Cruising through Orlando

The four regions I've chosen to cover – Orlando, Tampa/St Petersburg, Miami, and Key West – are the most popular tourist areas in Florida. They each have unique features and differ greatly in character. You can easily spend three to four days in each area without getting bored. Driving times between the regions depend on the routes taken and whether you want to ramble leisurely or concentrate on getting from point A to point B. To help you plan your itineraries, a general guideline is: Orlando to Tampa takes about 1½ hours, Tampa to Miami about 4 hours, Miami to Key West about 3 hours. The tours in this guide start in the center of the state, then head toward the west coast, cross over to the southeast, and end in the southernmost portion of the state. Read through the following selections, pick the places that you just must see, plan a route that suits your schedule, and get started on your Florida vacation.

RARIES

ORLANDO AREA

Once upon a time, before there was Disney, there was Orlando – a small patch of commerce amid the vast orange groves of central Florida. But when Mickey Mouse made his debut in 1971 things changed. Tourists began arriving in record numbers, and in the years that followed dozens of other major attractions opened, turning Orlando's small-town atmosphere into a thing of the past. But even though the Orlando area is considered to be the most-visited commercial tourist destination in the world, in the heart of it all there is still the city itself. Today, Orlando is a beautiful metropolitan area with a blend of stately, old homes and modern skyscrapers.

1. The City of Orlando

A day tour through the city of Orlando offers a real-world glimpse of what life in Central Florida is all about. A comfortable itinerary can include a morning visit to the city's museum complex at Loch Haven Park, or a visit to the lush Leu Gardens, and then lunch and some late afternoon entertainment at Church Street Station.

Although the population in the Orlando area has now reached almost one million, the downtown district has maintained an old-fashioned,

Orlando's Lake Eola

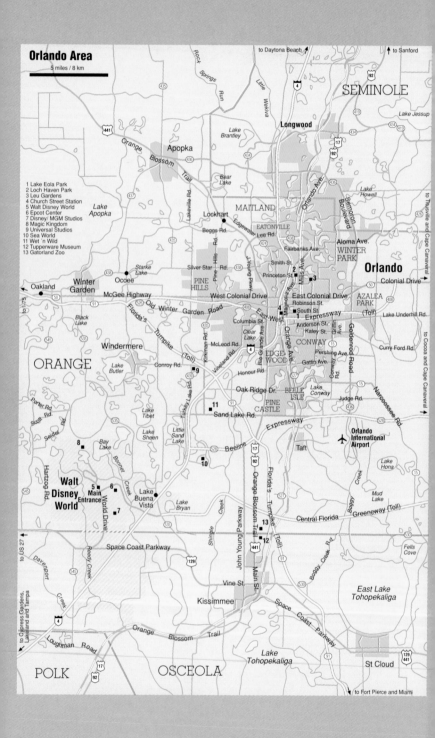

Orlando Area

5 miles / 8 km

1 Lake Eola Park
2 Loch Haven Park
3 Leu Gardens
4 Church Street Station
5 Walt Disney World
6 Epcot Center
7 Disney/ MGM Studios
8 Magic Kingdom
9 Universal Studios
10 Sea World
11 Wet 'n Wild
12 Tupperware Museum
13 Gatorland Zoo

Bloom in Leu Gardens

pastoral feeling. At the center of the city is Lake Eola Park, a peaceful spread of land surrounded by Mediterranean-style homes with jogging trails and bike paths. Locals and tourists congregate in the park for morning walks and afternoon picnics, or a paddleboat ride on the lake. In the evenings, horse-drawn carriages are available for a gentle spin around the grounds.

To the north of Orlando's downtown district, off Mills Avenue, is **Loch Haven Park**. An expanse of red brick pathways and moss-draped oak trees, the Park offers a choice of four museums. For history buffs, the **Orange County Historical Museum** (Tuesday to Friday 10am–4pm, Saturday and Sunday 1–5pm), holds a substantial collection of exhibits on the area's history. The **Orlando Science Center** (Monday to Thursday 9am–5pm, Friday 9am–9pm, Saturday noon–9pm, Sunday noon–5pm) offers a variety of educational science exhibits along with a planetarium. Model train collectors will enjoy **Fire Station No. 3** (Tuesday to Friday 10am–4pm, Saturday and Sunday 1–5pm), the city's oldest standing fire station (built in 1926), where antique fire-fighting equipment and memorabilia are displayed. For art-lovers, the **Orlando Fine Arts Museum** (Tuesday to Friday 10am–5pm, Saturday and Sunday 1–5pm) houses a sophisticated collection of both classic and contemporary art. Most museums charge a small entrance fee, but parking in Loch Haven Park is free.

If you'd rather spend your morning outdoors, drive a few miles west of the downtown area on North Forest Avenue until you see the sign for **Leu Gardens** (Tuesday to Saturday 10am–4pm, Sunday and Monday 1–4pm), a 56-acre botanical park full of roses, camellias, palms and azaleas. Once a private estate, Leu Gardens was transformed by its owners into a Central Florida horticultural showplace and educational center. The peaceful grounds feel like a Zen retreat and include an orchid conservatory, a formal European-style rose garden, a native wetland garden, a ravine and waterfalls, and a cacti collection. The former private home on the grounds is now a museum where lectures on herbal wines, spice growing, butterfly gardening, and natural perfume-making are held.

When you're ready for lunch, drive toward the downtown area south of Lake Eola Park, and find a parking space in one of the public lots near Church Street. Once you're on Church Street you won't be able to miss the city's liveliest and most popular attraction. **Church Street Station** (daily 11am–2am) is a dazzling

Stop at Church Street Station

A pick-me-up on ice

emporium of shops, shows, restaurants, bars and dance halls. Although the admission charge is a bit high, it includes live entertainment and entrance into all the attractions. Once you get into the mood of the place, you'll likely want to stay for the evening floor shows.

Opened in the 1970s by an adventurous bi-plane pilot, Church Street Station has grown from the small and funky **Rosie O'Grady's Good Time Emporium** that still exists today to a massive entertainment complex that includes high-kicking dancing girls, ragtime music, hearty food, generously poured drinks, and Victorian antiques. For lunch, try the **Cheyenne Barbecue Restaurant**. The barbecue beef ribs and chicken are great; so are the hefty buffalo-burgers.

After eating, take a walk and explore: **Phineas Phogg's Balloon Works**, Church Street Station's most popular disco/dance club-cum-ballooning museum with artifacts from historic balloon flights; the **Cheyenne Saloon and Opera House**, a recreation of a Western-style saloon with wooden Indians and an antique gun collection, or the **Church Street Railroad Depot**, an antique railroad car surrounded by a parade of pushcart vendors.

2. Walt Disney World

The granddaddy of all Florida theme parks, **Walt Disney World** is located about 20 miles south of Orlando in Lake Buena Vista off I-4. From the interstate highway three exits lead into the 27,000-acre resort. The first takes you into the Disney hotel complex, the second into EPCOT Center, and the third into the Magic Kingdom and Disney-MGM Studios. Each parking lot is as big as a small

Earffel Tower

town so don't worry about finding a space. A sleek monorail makes getting around easy. Since all three main Disney attractions are enormous, it's impossible (or at least insane) to try to visit more than one in a day.

Crowd control is one of the things Disney is famous for, so be prepared for long, but well-organized and fast-moving queues. Cameras, baby carriages and wheel-chairs are available for rent, as are lockers to store gifts or bags that you don't want to carry.

Hours

Disney World is open 365 days a year, but hours vary according to the time of year and holiday schedules – all attractions officially open at 9am, but you can enter the grounds at 8am. Closing times, however, vary from 6pm to 10pm, depending on the attraction. For current operating hours and general information on all of the Disney World attractions call 407-824 4321. The busiest days of the week are Monday, Tuesday and Wednesday; the slowest are Friday and Sunday.

Admission

Admission tickets come in two categories: adult – anyone over 10, and children – ages 3–9. Children under three get in free. Tickets are sold in one-day, four-day, five-day, or six-day passes and include admission to all exhibits and rides. The one-day tickets entitle you to enter one of the three attractions. The others grant you entrance into all of the attractions and unlimited use of the on-property Disney transportation system. Some of the theme parks inside the three attractions offer separate, one-day admission rates.

Tickets can be purchased at the attractions' entrance booths, several Orlando area hotels, and the Orlando International Airport. If you need to leave one of the Disney attractions and plan on returning that same day, you must have your hand stamped before you depart in order to be able to get back in. A day at Disney World is not cheap – count on spending at least $55 per adult and $45 per child for entrance costs and meals, and a few dollars for parking your car.

Magic Kingdom

The **Magic Kingdom** is where you'll find most of the Mickey Mouse action. Its 98 acres of enchanting fantasyland are a maze of over 45

Mickey, Minnie, Goofy and Donald go for a ride

A match made in fantasyland

attractions and dozens of restaurants and shops. The entranceway takes you right through **Main Street, USA,** a wholesome and happy rendition of small-town America with a City Hall, Town Square and horse-drawn trolleys. At the **Main Street Cinema,** vintage Disney cartoons are shown continuously. Directly past Main Street are the majestic spires of **Cinderella Castle** (designed to resemble King Ludwig's castle in Bavaria), the Magic Kingdom's hub. At the castle's entrance is a series of mosaic murals that tells the tale of the poor little cinder girl and her fairy godmother.

Although there's no dungeon beneath the castle, there is a secret labyrinth of service tunnels that is used to haul the tons of trash produced by the Kingdom daily.

Across the bridge on the west side of the castle is **Adventureland,** a series of exotic attractions and rides that includes **Pirates of the Caribbean** (a cruise through a simulated pirate raid), **Swiss Family Treehouse,** and the **Jungle Cruise.** Nearby is **Frontierland,** a recreation of the American Frontier from the 1770s through the 1880s with a shooting arcade, jail, cemetery, and a scream-your-lungs-out roller-coaster ride.

Liberty Square, another enclave, has the spooky and very **Haunted Mansion,** the **Liberty Square Riverboat** rides, and the **Hall of Presidents** – a rather dry attraction that appeals to only the most dedicated history buffs.

Fantasyland, on the east side of the Cinderella Castle, is a collection of storybook rides – the **Mad Tea Party, Dumbo the Flying Elephant,** and **Peter Pan's Flight** – which appeal to young children. At **Mickey Mouse at Starland** you can visit a place called **Duckburg** and have your picture taken at Mickey's house. **Tomorrowland** – an educational but for the most part humdrum glimpse of the future – is where you'll find **Space Mountain,** a thrilling, space-age roller-coaster that takes you in the dark past shooting stars.

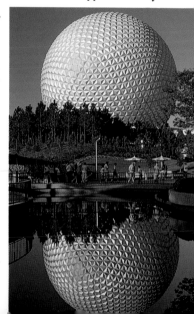

The EPCOT Center

EPCOT Center

Divided into two distinct attractions, **EPCOT Center** is one part modern technology showcase and one part world fair. An acronym for Environmental Prototype Community of Tomorrow, EPCOT was Walter Elias Disney's deathbed dream.

Future World, EPCOT's modern technology part, occupies the southern half of the 260-acre park. Themes include energy, communications, transportation, oceanography and agriculture. Although educational, the attractions are sponsored by American corporate giants and are therefore not lacking in promotional messages. At the center of the complex is **Spaceship Earth**, a 17-story high, silver geosphere with a ride that takes you on a historic journey from the days of Cro-Magnon man up to the present. **Horizons** is a display on life styles of the future with robots and space cities, **The Living Seas** examines marine life on the planet, and **Wonders of Life** looks at the wonders of the human body.

Across the 40-acre lagoon from Future World is the **World Showcase**, a promenade of pavilions dedicated to the history, art, music and foods of cultures around the world. France, Morocco, Japan, Italy, Germany, Norway, Mexico, China and the US are all represented in individual pavilions. Natives from the countries serve as hosts, and the gift shops sell indigenous crafts. Some of the displays include a sidewalk Paris café, a Munich-style beer hall, and an Aztec-inspired Mexican pyramid. Although an air-conditioned Tangier bazaar and an antiseptically clean Beijing neighborhood are a bit too synthetic to feel like the real thing, the pavilions are an ethnic treat and do provide a taste of the countries for those who have never visited them.

Disney-MGM Studios

The last of the three Disney giants is **Disney-MGM Studios**, a working television and film studio as well as theme park. The studio's **Backstage Studio Tour** and **Animation Tour** are perfect for film buffs who want a behind-the-scenes lesson in special effects, scenery and sound production, and costuming. The **Great Movie Ride** is an animated tour through movie sets with John Wayne on horseback, Gene Kelly singing in the rain, Tarzan's jungle cry, Dorothy and her friends dancing down the Yellow Brick Road, and the tearful farewell scene from *Casablanca*. The **Twilight Zone Tower of Terror** has become one of the most exciting and popular scare rides, on an elevator that 'crashes' with all aboard. Inspired by Spielberg's *Star Wars*, **Star Tours** is a rollicking tour through outerspace; it is a rough ride that is not recommended for people with back problems, heart conditions, or motion sickness.

MGM Studios

3. Other Theme Parks

If you have an extra day after a trip to Disney, and are still in the mood for make-believe, then consider planning a day tour to one of the many other attractions in the area. All of them have fairly good restaurants on the premises and, like Disney, they can easily take up an entire day.

One of the newest is **Universal Studios Florida** (daily 9am–6pm), a television and film studio similar to the Disney-MGM Studios. Admission fees are about the same as at Disney, but as this is the largest studio outside Hollywood the entertainment is even better. The entrance is 1½ miles north of I-4 on Kirkman Road.

The 40 or more sets include the bustling sidewalks of New York City, San Francisco's Fisherman's Wharf, a charming New England village, and the garden of Allah. The rides and shows let you escape an attack by King Kong, feel the violent rumble of an earthquake, take a boat ride past the 24-ft killer shark from *Jaws*, and be a witness

Refueling at Universal Studios

to the frightening shower scene from Alfred Hitchcock's *Psycho*. You can also take a screen test and star in your own *Star Trek* video, meet the friendly alien E.T., and take a lesson in the gory techniques of horror movie make-up. After a day spent at Universal Studios, eat at the **Hard Rock Café**, located within the Universal property. Part of the worldwide chain known for its rock music memorabilia, it serves excellent cheeseburgers and other north American favorites.

Wet 'n' Wild (June to September daily 9am–9pm, October to May 10am–5pm, closed January to mid-February) on International Drive not far from Universal Studios, is a 25-acre water theme park that offers water slides, flumes, floats and plunges. Here you can spend an entire day in your bathing suit and never once want to dry off. If you're not a good swimmer you need not worry, as the water depths never exceed standing height and there are always lifeguards on duty. You can ride 4-ft waves in a simulated surfing lagoon, raft through white-water rapids, free-fall down a 250-ft slide, and water-ski on a knee board or inner tube around a fresh-

Dolphin-power at Sea World

water lake. Admission fees are moderate and there are plenty of food kiosks where you can create your own picnic.

Just south of Wet 'n' Wild at the intersection of I-4 and the Bee Line Expressway is the largest marine park in the world, **Sea World** (daily 9am–7pm). Another all-day attraction, Sea World is on a par with Disney World when it comes to putting on an elaborate show. Admission fees are moderate and the well-organized park offers all the amenities a family might need. Although lying an hour's drive from the nearest bit of coast, Sea World makes you feel as if you are in the middle of the Atlantic Ocean.

The 5,000-lb star of the show is **Shamu the Killer Whale** who performs her jumps, flips and kisses while drenching a mesmerized audience. Other popular performers include sea-lions, penguins, dolphins, otters, and a gregarious walrus. One of Sea World's more educational exhibits is the shark tank, where you can learn all about the ominous creatures and watch as they indulge in a bloody feeding frenzy. Other exhibits include a feeding pool where you can drop a herring into the mouth of a passing seal, and a trip inside a research submarine. In the evenings, Sea World hosts a Polynesian-style luau dinner show complete with hula dancers and fire jugglers.

A 40-minute drive south of Disney World, off I-4 in the town of **Winter Haven**, is a central Florida landmark. One of the oldest attractions in the state, **Cypress Gardens** (daily 9am–6pm) was founded during the Depression and has remained a Florida tourism staple ever since. The park's 223 acres of over 8,000 varieties of flowers and plants is one of the most lush botanical gardens in the world. Along with the beautiful young women dressed in ruffled hoop-skirts who wander around the property, Cypress Gardens is

known for its world-champion water-skiing shows, synchronized swimmers, and parrot and alligator shows.

One of the more offbeat attractions in Orlando is **Ripley's Believe It Or Not!** (daily 10am–midnight) on International Drive. Like the 20 other Ripley's museums in cities around the world, this one is also dedicated to the display of oddities and curiosities from far corners of the globe. Among its collection are a 20-ft segment of

Cypress Gardens, Winter Haven

the Berlin Wall, a gruesome pain and torture gallery, and a 20-ft high mural portrait of the artist Vincent van Gogh pieced together out of 3,000 postcards.

An Orlando attraction that lures those who love four-wheel play things is **Fun 'n' Wheels** (Monday to Friday 6–11pm, Saturday and Sunday 10am–11pm) on Sand Lake Road near International Drive. A no-nonsense park that offers bumper cars, go-cart rides, boats and miniature golf, Fun 'n' Wheels is a simple but entertaining kind of place where you pay only for the rides you want to try and nothing for admission. The **Mystery Fun House** (daily 10am–11pm), on Major Drive in Orlando, appeals to horror movie fans. Its 15-room mansion is full of moving floors, magic mirrors, and monsters who jump out of closets and try to grab you.

A good example of one of the only-in-Florida attractions is the **Tupperware Museum and International Headquarters** (Monday to Friday 9am–4pm) on US 441 on the southside of Orlando. A museum dedicated to those American-made, plastic food containers that make bored homemakers squeal with joy, the Tupperware Headquarters offers visitors a 25-minute guided tour that explains the history of food storage from early civilization to today. Its collection includes a food container that supposedly dates back to 4000BC, and an entire wing called the **Museum of Dishes**. Admission is free, and the museum could be a lifesaving alternative to staying in your hotel room on a rainy day.

4. Kissimmee

If you feel that you've had enough of the theme park scene, and want to escape for a day of reality, consider taking a drive south of Orlando for a day trip to the old-time Florida town of **Kissimmee**, wedged between the Florida Turnpike and I-4. Kissimmee is still a small place with quaint old homes, towering 100-year-old oak trees, and residents who still say good-morning to strangers. Once a busy station on the Seaboard Railroad line where small hotels attracted winter travelers, and saloons allowed cowboys to ride up on their horses for a shot of red-eye, Kissimmee fell into hard times after the state's highway system was put in place.

Home to the **Florida Cattleman's Association**, Kissimmee is where many of the state's livestock shows and cattle auctions take place, and it's also where hard-working ranch hands and the Florida cowboy rodeo crowd hang out. Kissimmee's annual **Silver Spurs Rodeo**, one of the nation's top 25 rodeos, takes place in February and July. For information about the Silver Spurs

Kissimmee cowboy

A cattleman takes stock

or other rodeos in the area call 407-847 5118. Cattle auctions are usually held on Wednesday.

Although most of the genuine old buildings were torn down years ago, the city's development council decided to bring some life back to town by creating what it calls the **Old Town** district. A manufactured enclave built to look like a 19th-century city, Old Town has a rustic, frontier look with brick-paved streets and several made-to-look-old antique shops. A good choice to stop for lunch in Kissimmee is **People's Place** on Broadway. Housed in a former blacksmith stable, People's Place offers a bargain-priced hot buffet prepared by students attending a nearby culinary school. The menus vary daily.

Star attraction, Gatorland

Across from the railroad station near the downtown district is Lake Front Park, where concerts and art shows take place. Inside the park is the **Monument of the States**, a 50-ft high statue made of 1,500 stones from all of the US states and 21 foreign countries. A garish conglomerate of marble, coral, platinum, agate and slate, the monument was designed by a local tourist club during World War II to represent their hope for world unity.

Not immune to the lure of the tourist dollar, Kissimmee also has a few bona fide tourist attractions. The **Gatorland Zoo** (open daily; September to May 8am–6pm, June to August 8am–8pm), on Orange Blossom Trail, confirms the fact that the mean-looking reptiles are

Tropical birds

no longer an endangered species in Florida. More than 4,000 alligators sleep in the sun on the shores of a muddy lake, and at feeding time jump out of the water to snap at dead chickens dangling from an overhead line. The zoo also features crocodiles, snakes, birds and alligator wrestling shows.

The **Flying Tigers Warbird Air Museum** (daily 9am–6pm), on Hoagland Boulevard, houses one of the finest collections of antique aircraft and aviation artifacts in the US. A working museum with restoration projects underway, the Warbird Museum charges a small admission fee that is worth the informative guided tour.

One of the most unusual attractions to be spawned by Mickey and friends is **Splendid China** (daily from 9.30am) set in a 76-acre park near Kissimmee. More than 60 of China's cultural, historical and natural sites are recreated in miniature, to scale, in the park (the Great Wall is 2,600-ft long). There are gift shops, of course, and live entertainment, especially jugglers, dancers, acrobats and martial artists.

5. Excursion to Kennedy Space Center

If you still have some time left during a visit to Central Florida, you might consider taking a day trip to the **Kennedy Space Center**, about a one-hour drive east of Orlando by way of the Bee Line Expressway and State Road 407.

Formerly called Cape Canaveral, the Kennedy Space Center is located on Merrit Island and is the launch base for America's space shuttle. The Center sprawls across 110,000 acres of heavily guarded, top-secret grounds where the ultimate in space technology is created. The goal of the center, according to National Aeronautics and Space Administration, is to carry out the peaceful exploration of outer space and the solar system through the use of communications satellites and automated spacecraft. Much of the land surrounding the center has been declared a National Wildlife Preserve and is part of the **Canaveral National Seashore**. A vast eco-system of plant life, birds, fish, alligators, wild pigs, deer and raccoons peacefully coexists in the mudflats and waterways adjacent to the modern technology that takes place right next door.

The visitor's center for tourists is **Spaceport USA** (daily 9am–dusk, closed Christmas) located one mile outside the Kennedy Space Center. A real-world Star Wars extravaganza that attracts over three million tourists a year, Spaceport USA offers a 2-hour educational bus tour into the Center with stops at the shuttle launch pads and the authentic Saturn V Moon Rocket. The **Satellites and You** exhibit is a state-of-the-art display where visitors can walk through a simulated space station. There are also tours from Spaceport USA that take you into the original Cape Canaveral site of the US Space Program from which Alan Shepard, the first US astronaut, blasted into space.

Exploration Station is a hands-on exhibit for children where they get to try on space suits and test their skills in outer space navigation. Other points of interest include the **Astronauts Hall of Fame** and the **Planetarium**. The **Astronauts Memorial** honors the 15 American astronauts who lost their lives in the line of duty. An array of exhibits in the grounds includes moon rocks, lunar rovers, telescopes, satellites and rockets. For lunch, the Spaceport USA cafeteria offers meals that make both children and adults happy.

During an actual launch, Spaceport USA is closed to the public, but it usually opens a few hours later. The launch schedule is irregular, so for upcoming dates and general information call 321-867 4636. Viewing a live blast-off can be a thrilling sensation (earplugs are suggested). You need not be right at the Center because the rockets can be seen and felt from many miles away. The best viewing spots are at Jetty Park in Cocoa Beach just south of the Center, and on Highway A1A along the Indian River. Parking and admission into Spaceport USA and all of its exhibits are free of charge; the bus tours into the Kennedy Space Center cost a few dollars. The entire Center takes about five hours to explore, and foreign language tapes are available for those who don't speak English. Since school groups take field trips to the Center during the week, weekends are usually less crowded.

Blast off!

Tampa/
St. Petersburg

While a long spell of sunny days is nothing special to brag about in Florida, the state's central west coast takes the prize when it comes to cloudless skies. Listed in the *Guinness Book of World Records* for the longest-ever run of consecutive sunny days – from 9 February 1967 to 17 March 1969 – the 25-mile stretch of soft-sand beaches nicknamed the Suncoast consistently lives up to its reputation.

Located about 75 miles southwest of Orlando off of Route 4, the twin cites of Tampa and St Petersburg are separated by the pretty, but polluted, Tampa Bay. Driving from the north or the south, the cities can be reached from I-75. One of the fastest growing regions in America, the urban area has a combined population of over 2 million. It also serves as the spring training-ground for several American major league baseball teams whose players get in shape and practise their sport at area stadiums.

6. Tampa

A full day spent exploring Tampa city, taking in the best museums, lunch on Harbor Island and the Latin American flavor of Ybor City.

The city of **Tampa**, part of Hillsborough County, is a dynamic metropolis that has a sophisticated and modern downtown center, and an ethnically rich historic quarter. A good way to plan a day tour of the city is to concentrate on the downtown area in the morning,

On the boardwalk, Tampa

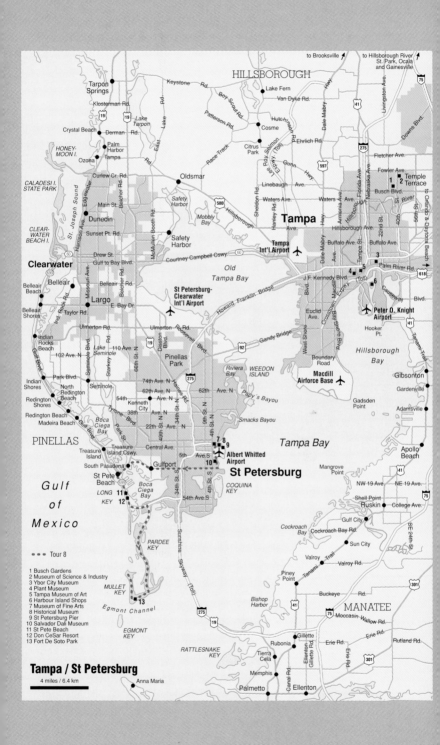

Tampa / St Petersburg

4 miles / 6.4 km

••• Tour 8

1 Busch Gardens
2 Museum of Science & Industry
3 Ybor City Museum
4 Plant Museum
5 Tampa Museum of Art
6 Harbour Island Shops
7 Museum of Fine Arts
8 Historical Museum
9 St Petersburg Pier
10 Salvador Dali Museum
11 St Pete Beach
12 Don CeSar Resort
13 Fort De Soto Park

perhaps picking a museum or two of interest, and then heading to Ybor City for a late-afternoon walk and dinner at a Cuban restaurant. Traffic in the downtown area is dense and driving can be difficult. Once you get there, and have decided which spots you want to visit, it's best to leave your car at one of the many public parking lots and walk through the city.

The heart of the downtown business district lies along the banks of the **River Hillsborough**, not far from the **Port of Tampa**, and within a few square miles there are several points of interest. Within walking distance from the **University of Tampa** campus, the **Henry B Plant Museum** (Tuesday to Saturday 10am–4pm, Sunday noon–4pm) on West Kennedy Boulevard is the only museum in the country housed in a former hotel. Henry B Plant was a railroad tycoon who was instrumental in the development of Tampa in the mid-1800s. The five-story museum once featured a casino, two grand ballrooms and an indoor swimming-pool. Today, it serves as a showcase for Plant's personal collection of Victorian art, furniture and fashion. Donations to the museum are invited.

The banks of the Hillsborough

A short walk over the river from the museum on Doyle Carlton Drive is the **Tampa Museum of Art** (Monday, Tuesday and Thursday to Saturday 10am–5pm, Wednesday 10am–9pm, Sunday 1–5pm), one of Florida's best art museums. The museum presents 15 changing exhibits yearly as well as a permanent collection of over 7,000 art works that include classic Greek and Roman antiquities, Egyptian artifacts and modern American art. There is a small admission fee, and the museum can easily take up an hour or two.

A few blocks away, at 711 Franklin Street Mall, a pedestrian-only brick street, one of the country's few remaining grand old single-screen cinemas, **The Tampa Theater**, still offers foreign and art films on a weekly basis, in addition to occasional live entertainment (call 813-274 8981). This theater still has its tall pillars, curved box seats, a balcony and even an organ that rises from the basement – all under a ceiling of painted clouds and twinkling stars. Beautifully restored in the Florida-Mediterranean style, the theater was built in 1926. Movies are usually shown on weekends.

If you're traveling with children (or other adults) who yawn at art museums, your morning might be better spent at the **Museum of Science and Industry** (Sunday to Thursday 9am–5pm, Friday and Saturday 9am–7pm) at the north end of the city on East

36

Fowler Avenue. One of the largest science centers in the southeast, the museum includes a planetarium, a 2,000 sq ft butterfly garden, and exhibits dedicated to scientific inventions. Children who pour their souls into creating their 6th grade science projects adore it.

Alternatively, one of Tampa's lesser known treasures is **The Florida Aquarium** (daily 9am–6pm) at 701 Channelside Drive, right on the city's busy waterfront. The newest West Coast attraction, the Aquarium features fishes of all shape and stripe – more than 4,300 varieties – including sharks and stingrays, and the million-gallon Coral Reefs Gallery is fascinating. When you've had enough or lunch time rolls around, you can nip across (by car, boat or Tampa's downtown people-mover train) to the Harbor Island shopping and restaurants complex.

After lunch, take a stroll through **Ybor City**. An ethnic enclave full of old character, Ybor City is actually a neighborhood rather than a real city. It's located in the northwest corner of Tampa and is bounded by Columbus Drive, Fifth Avenue, Nebraska Avenue and 22nd Street. The 110-block area is one of the three national landmark districts in Florida.

Founded in 1886 by Don Vicente Martinez Ybor, a wealthy Cuban tobacco merchant, Ybor City attracted cigar factory workers from Key West and Cuba in the late 1800s and early 1900s. In its heyday, its 50 cigar factories employed over 40,000 workers and was known as the 'Cigar Capital of the World'. The area was a lively business district where recent immigrants – Cubans, Spaniards, Italians, Germans and Jews – all worked together. Although an ethnically mixed neighborhood, Ybor City's Hispanic character was, and still is, dominant. Shop owners lived above their stores, talked to their neighbors from their balconies, and socialized at the many casinos and speakeasies. But the austere years of the Depression, and the sacrifices of World War II, brought hard times to Ybor City. Factories closed down and families moved away. In the years that followed it fell deeper and deeper into decay. Many of the buildings were demolished, and derelicts took up residence in others.

But the seeds of a Ybor City revitalization plan were planted in the late 1970s, and Tampa was determined to bring back its beautiful historic treasure. Old cigar factories were turned into shopping centers and restaurants, and much of the architecture was restored. The red brick streets were improved and the old gas street lights refurbished. These days, the district appears almost like it did in the good-old-days, with ornate grillwork and Spanish-style architecture.

Cuban lady

Tourists flock to its streets, as do locals who come by for drinks after work. If you arrive early enough you can catch one of the free walking tours (offered Tuesday, Thursday and Saturday at 1.30pm) that depart from the **Ybor Square's Visitor Center** on 14th Street, Tel: 813-223 1111. If you miss the tour, pick up a free walking-tour map at the center and wander around on our own. Next door to the visitor's center is **Ybor Square** (Monday to Saturday 9.30am–5.30pm, Sunday noon–5.30pm), the former site of the original Ybor Cigar Factory and now a shopping center with vintage clothing boutiques, customized jewelry shops, art galleries, and Cuban grocery stores and cafés. Walk two blocks south of Ybor Square and you'll be on 7th Avenue. Here you will find **El Sol Cigars** (Monday to Saturday 9am–5pm) where you can pick up a box of thick, hand-rolled Cuban cigars, and the **El Molino Coffee Shop** (Monday to Saturday 9am–5pm) where you can buy sacks of strong Cuban coffee roasted on the premises.

In Ybor City

Continue walking down 7th Avenue until you come to 18th Street. To your right will be the **Italian Club**, a social center for Ybor's Italian-American community. Turn left on 18th Street and walk two blocks until you get to Ninth Avenue and you will see the massive brick structure that houses the **Ybor City State Museum** (Tuesday to Saturday 9am–noon and 1–5pm). The former Ferlita Bakery building built in 1923, the museum complex includes three restored cigar workers' homes where the smell of tobacco still permeates the air. It offers a walk-through history lesson on Ybor City full of historic photos and artifacts from the cigar industry.

No visit to Ybor City is complete without a robust, Spanish-style meal. The neighborhood favorite, and supposedly the oldest restaurant in Florida, founded in 1905, is the **Columbia Restaurant** (daily 11am–10pm) on 7th Avenue. With an ornate European decor including hand-painted tiles, the Columbia's specialty is a saffron-rich *paella* accompanied by a salad of lettuce, ham, cheese, olives and lots of garlic. And to liven up your spirit after a long day in Tampa, it also features the rhythmic stomping of an authentic flamenco floor show.

Busch inhabitants

7. Busch Gardens

A full-day 'African Safari'.

Although Tampa has a lot to offer, the main reason most tourists make a trip to the city is to visit **Busch Gardens** (daily 9.30am–6pm, extended hours in summer). Located about 8 miles northeast of downtown Tampa, 2 miles west of I-75 on exit 54, the 300-acre theme park is one of the best in the state. Ranked as one of the finest zoos in the US, Busch Gardens is a miniature Africa (but clean, man-made and well-organized, of course).

Opened in 1959 as a small-scale zoo and attraction, Busch Gardens in recent years has been transformed into a competitor of Disney World. Admission fees are expensive but include access to all the exhibits and rides; parking is a few dollars more. There are many restaurants to choose from. Plan on devoting an entire day to see the attractions, and be prepared to leave exhausted. Wear comfortable clothes that you don't mind getting wet.

As if on an African safari, you can roam around the grounds and view more than 3,000 animals, birds, and reptiles representing over 300 species. The park is divided into several theme regions. The **Serengeti Plain** is an 80-acre flatland where herds of antelope, giraffes, black rhinos and Asian elephants roam free. Visitors can view the animals from an elevated monorail or steam locomotive. **Stanleyville** is a recreation of an African village where you can take a ride on the **Tanganyika Tidal Wave**. The **Congo** exhibit, home to rare white Bengal tigers, offers a feisty white-water raft ride down the 'Congo River'. The **Morocco** exhibit features an exotic walled city, palace, snake charmers and Marrakesh theater. Other attractions include a roller-coaster, an elephant preserve, a koala habitat, an animal nursery, an exotic bird garden, ice-skating shows, and country music extravaganzas.

A pregnant mother rests

8. St Petersburg

A full day in the St Petersburg area, with breakfast on the Municipal Pier, a visit to the Salvador Dalí Museum and an afternoon on the beaches of the Suncoast.

A narrow peninsula with Tampa Bay to the east and the calm Gulf of Mexico to the west, the city of **St Petersburg** and its broad beaches is both a retirement community and vacation playground. It can be reached from Tampa by four causeways; all have signs leading you to the downtown or beach areas. If you have only a day to spend in St Petersburg, prepare to make it a long one.

The downtown district is along the bayside of the city and most of the downtown attractions are adjacent to the St Petersburg **Municipal Pier** (daily 10am–9pm). A long, runway-like road leads out to The Pier's main building – a five-story, inverted pyramid structure with a panoramic view of Tampa Bay. A huge parking lot at the foot of the pier charges you a few dollars to leave your car for the day, but admission to the pier is free.

Originally a railroad pier built in 1889, the new pier was rebuilt in 1973 and then turned into a festive marketplace in 1988. It's full of gift shops, art galleries, a unique vertical aquarium, restaurants and cafés. Musicians, mimes and jugglers regularly entertain the crowds as seagulls and pelicans soar overhead. The fresh muffins and cappuccino are worth an early-morning visit.

The marina on the east side of The Pier has hundreds of sailboats – some for rent – and the surrounding waters are a popular place for jet-ski races. On the north side of the entrance to the pier, on NE 2nd Avenue, is the **St Petersburg Historical Museum** (Tuesday to Saturday 10am–5pm, Sunday 1–5pm). The museum displays changing exhibits on St Petersburg and Florida history. Across the street on Beach Drive you will find the **Museum of Fine Arts** (Tuesday to Saturday 10am–5pm, Sunday 1–5pm) where a fine collection of American, French Impressionist, Far Eastern and pre-Columbian art is displayed. A small donation is suggested.

But if you have only one museum visit on your day's agenda, you're better off making your choice the **Salvador Dalí Museum**

Entrance to the Arts

St Petersburg Beach

(Tuesday to Saturday 9.30am–5.30pm, Sunday noon–5.30pm). To get there, drive east on 2nd Avenue from the pier and turn left again on 3rd Street. At the end of the street you will see the large white museum. One of the finest art centers in the country, the museum, opened in 1982, houses a permanent exhibit that you would expect to find in New York, Madrid, or Paris. The collection consists of some of the Spanish surrealist's finest and most famous works including 93 oil paintings, 200 watercolors and drawings, and 1,000 prints. It is said to be the largest collection of his work in the world. Narrated tours of the museum, including a life history of Dalí, are offered at intervals throughout the day, and the gift shop sells signed lithographs, wall-posters, and some cleverly designed melting watches.

If you have time on your way to the beach, you might want to check out one of the things St Petersburg is famous for – very serious shuffleboard competitions. Yes, pushing those clay disks with a long stick so that they land in the highest scoring spot on the board is an art form in St Petersburg, and the city has the **National Shuffleboard Hall of Fame** (Monday to Friday 9am–1pm) to prove it. To get there, retrace the drive back to the pier and head east on 2nd Avenue until you come to Mirror Lake Drive. As part of the **St Petersburg Shuffleboard Club** – the oldest and largest shuffleboard club in the country – the Hall of Fame is a hokey shrine to some of the city's finest shufflers. There is no admission fee and the director of the club is happy to take you on a tour and personally explain the history of the sport.

By mid-afternoon you'll be ready for lunch and a stroll, or swim, along the **Gulf Beaches**. Several causeways take you westward from the downtown area to the long string of beaches that includes several seaside communities as well as St Pete Beach. Most of the beach towns have so far resisted the onslaught of high-rise hotels and condominiums that have almost enveloped most of the eastern Florida coast. Instead, the Suncoast beaches are packed with small, mom-and-pop motels, casual restaurants, and easy-going playgrounds.

From the northern to the southernmost tip of the beach strip, **Gulf Boulevard** is the main thoroughfare that passes through the towns of Clearwater, Indian Rocks Beach, Madeira Beach, Treasure Island and then finally **St Pete Beach**. For lunch, stop off at **Cracker's Bar and Grill** on Gulf Boulevard overlooking St Pete Beach. Some of the best choices on Cracker's menu include fried alligator, grilled dolphin fish, raw oysters and Creole jambalaya.

The Don CeSar Hotel

When you're through eating, you'll probably welcome a beach walk. Aside from small parking fees, access to the beaches is free. The **St Pete Municipal Beach** is a broad beach with clumps of wild sea-oats, dressing-rooms and snack bars. Volley-ball games and kite-flying are popular, as are para-sail rides from offshore speed-boats. Although the Gulf beaches about 100 miles to the south are the best places in Florida for finding seashells, the St Petersburg area is also good for shelling.

If you continue driving on Gulf Boulevard south of the Municipal Beach, you'll see the ornate, pink rococo palace known as the **Don CeSar Beach Resort** on your right. Built in the 1920s, the grand old hotel was once a favorite hideaway of author F Scott Fitzgerald, and during its first incarnation was the epitome of ostentatious living. But decades later it fell into ruins and by 1971 it was an embarrassing eyesore. A total restoration was completed in the 1980s, and the Don CeSar is once again the first-class, flamingo-pink beauty of its past. You don't have to be a hotel guest to wander around the pool or take a peek inside the hotel where antique shops, fancy boutiques and art galleries dot the lobby.

A few miles south of the Don CeSar is **Fort De Soto Park** (open sunrise to sunset), one of the most pristine and natural beaches on the central Gulf Coast. South of St Pete Beach, Fort De Soto can be reached by taking Gulf Boulevard east to the Pinellas Bayway and then driving south. Access to the park and parking is free, but a highway toll booth charges a small fee.

The 900-acre park, made up of six islands, is a historic site that dates back to the Spanish-American War. You can wander around the old fort that once protected the coast from Spanish fleets, and watch huge tankers make their way into Tampa Bay. In addition to the quiet, isolated beaches, the park has a fishing pier, picnic areas, dressing facilities, and a camp ground. Lush mangroves, dotted with water birds, surround the park grounds that are now a wildlife refuge.

In the summer months porpoises often play in the waters near to shore, and swimmers can get close to them. In the evening, sunsets range from pale pink to a Bloody Mary red.

A Florida flamingo checks her chick

Miami

Miami conjures up many images in the mind of the traveler: drug-smuggling cowboys, beautiful women, rainbow-colored skyscrapers, old Art Deco hotels, and thousands of Cuban immigrants. As one of America's most unique and interesting cities, Miami's exotic persona never fails to amuse.

Situated inside Dade County and bordered by the Atlantic Ocean, Greater Miami contains 28 different municipalities and has

a total population of about 2 million. More than half of its residents are foreign-born, making it feel more South American or Caribbean than American. Being able to speak a little Spanish, although not essential, frequently comes in handy here.

Much of Miami's hustle-bustle activity takes place in the heart of its downtown district. It is here that shoppers from cities as far afield as Caracas, Bogotá, Nassau and Kingston regularly come to stock up on supplies. It is also where Miami's thriving international banking industry and the busy cruise and commercial port are be found.

The fresh face of Art Deco

9. Downtown Miami

A full day in downtown Miami, beginning with the boutiques and art galleries at Biscayne Bay. Afterwards an orientating ride on the Metromover and a walk down Flagler Street, passing some fine examples of Art Deco architecture, to the Metro-Dade Cultural Plaza.

The best place to start a day tour of downtown Miami is from **Bayside Marketplace** (daily 9am–midnight) located on the water at Biscayne Boulevard. Entrance to the marketplace is free, but parking costs a few dollars. Bayside is a 16-acre shopping and entertainment complex of restaurants, bars, boutiques, kiosks, and art galleries. Hopping with action from morning till night, Bayside can easily take about four hours to explore. Live music – salsa, jazz, reggae, and pop – continuously floats through the air, and an array of boats – catamarans, gondolas, sailboats – is available for those who want to take a quick sail around Biscayne Bay. One of the more distinctive shops in the complex is Art by God, a gallery that specializes in animal bones, fossils, mounted fish, antlers, shark jaws, bear-skin rugs and primitive art. Although not the kind of place to make an animal rights advocate happy, it is one of the more unusual stores to be found in the Miami area.

Bayside

Exiting Bayside Marketplace you will find yourself facing a peach-colored Mediterranean Revival building to the north on

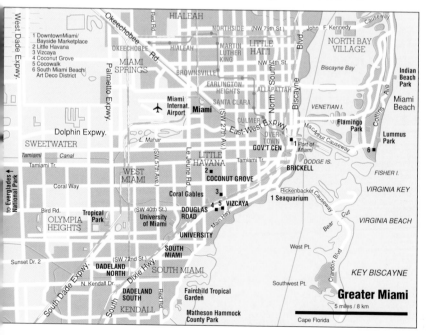

Biscayne Boulevard known as the **Freedom Tower**. Built in 1925, the Freedom Tower was once the home of the now defunct *Miami News*, but acquired its name during the 1960s when it served as the processing center for Cuban refugees who were seeking freedom in Miami. To the south of Bayside Marketplace, also on Biscayne Boulevard, is **Bayfront Park**, a large breeze-filled playground that is often used for outdoor musical events and ethnic festivals. At the eastern edge of the park is a statue of Christopher Columbus given to the city of Miami by the Italian government in 1953. At the southern end of the park is a modern-looking memorial, designed by the late Japanese sculptor Isamu Noguchi, that honors the astronauts and crew who perished when the space shuttle *Challenger* exploded in 1986.

Waiting for a gold rush

For a quick orientation of downtown Miami, take a ride on the **Metromover**. Although designed to make getting around downtown easy, the Metromover is popular with tourists who want a bird's-eye view of the city. After crossing Biscayne Boulevard walk west on NE 4th Street about two blocks and you will find the College/Bayside Metromover Station. Deposit 25¢ in the turnstile, walk up the stairs and board the little green and white train. Both the inner and outer loop rides will take you on a 10-minute jaunt through downtown and eventually return you to the same station. One of the buildings to be on the lookout for is the 47-story, three-tiered **International Place**. Formerly called CenTrust Tower, the building at night takes on a spectacular look because of a series of colored lights on its facade. Sometimes it is pink, sometimes it is blue, and sometimes it is a kaleidoscope of colors.

After the short train tour, exit down the stairs and continue walking west on NE 4th Street until you come to NE 2nd Avenue and turn left. You will be facing the Wolfson Campus of Miami-Dade Community College, one of the largest community colleges in the US. Walk four blocks south until you come to East Flagler Street and turn right. Flagler Street, the main commercial artery, is full of electronic, jewelry, and clothing stores. Although congested and a bit run-down, it is a good place to do some bargain shopping. On Flagler you will also find the **Gusman Center for the Performing Arts**, an ornate Spanish-style theater built for

Paramount Pictures in the 1920s. A little further on Flagler is the **Alfred I duPont Building**, a classic Art Deco office building put up in the 1930s. And at 38 East Flagler Street is the **Flagler Station Mall** (Monday to Saturday 10am–6pm), an enclosed shopping center that houses the small but special **Floridita Restaurant**. Famous in Cuba before its owners migrated to Miami, the Floridita is a good place to stop for a pastry and cup of Cuban coffee.

About a block past the Floridita is the **Dade County Courthouse**, a massive, neoclassical structure built in the 1920s. The Courthouse is one of downtown's busiest buildings and a favorite gathering spot for Miami lawyers. At the major intersection to the west of the Courthouse, East Flagler becomes West Flagler Street. Crossing to West Flagler, you will find the **Metro-Dade Cultural Plaza**. Follow the ramp alongside the flowing pools of water and you will find yourself in the plaza's main courtyard, a grand, Italian-style piazza popular at lunchtime with the downtown office crowd. There's a convenient refreshment stand on the plaza.

Exploring the three buildings that make up the plaza is a great way to spend a downtown afternoon when the heat of the city is at its most intense. The first building is the **Miami-Dade Public Library** (Monday to Thursday 8am–9pm, Friday 8am–4.30pm, Saturday 9am–1pm), home to the county library system's largest collection of books and videos including an entire wing devoted to Miami and Florida. Since admission is free, the library often attracts local homeless people who come in to cool off, but their presence just adds a little color to the place. In the center of the plaza is the **Historical Museum of Southern Florida** (Monday to Wednesday, Friday and Saturday 10am–5pm, Thursday 10am–9pm,

Sunday noon–5pm; small admission fee). The museum explains the history of South Florida from the days when Native Americans lived on the banks of the Miami River to the present. Its collection includes an old Miami trolley-car and lots of historic artifacts depicting the mass exodus of Cuban exiles to Miami. The museum gift shop sells Seminole Indian crafts and local art works. The last point of interest is the **Miami Art Museum** (Tuesday to Friday 10am–5pm, Saturday and Sunday noon–5pm; small admission fee), one of the best art museums in the state, with classical and modern art.

The Metro-Dade Cultural Plaza

Breakfast at the News Café followed by a tour of Miami's historic Art Deco district.

In the past 10 years, Miami Beach – more specifically South Miami Beach – has established itself as the trendy get-away of celebrities, European photographers, and in-the-know beautiful people. Its reputation as America's Riviera is not unfounded, and it is without a doubt one of Florida's must-see places.

At the southern tip of the barrier island that is Miami Beach, South Beach is a dense neighborhood of whimsical architecture, casual outdoor cafés and a bustling street life. It's a delightful place for a walking tour and can easily be reached from Miami proper by way of the MacArthur Causeway. As you drive east along the causeway you will see the behemoth cruise ships that line the docks of the Port of Miami, the largest cruise port in the world.

South Miami Beach

As the causeway ends it becomes 5th Street and you will pass the Miami Beach Marina on your right. Continue driving east until you come to Ocean Drive and turn left. This is the beginning of the historic Art Deco District which runs from 6th to 23rd streets along the ocean, and west to Alton Road. The largest collection of Art Deco architecture in the world, the district includes over 500 Deco structures, some perfectly preserved, others in dilapidated shape. In recent years the district has become a favorite location for fashion shoots so be prepared for dozens of long-legged models lounging around in front of the quirky pastel-colored buildings.

A good spot to start a tour of South Beach (SoBe as it is called by locals) is at the **News Café** (daily 24-hours) on Ocean Drive and 8th Street. The News is a combination Eu-

Volleyball: a favorite beach pursuit

ropean café, newsstand and jazz club. One of the hottest places on the beach, it is always busy and getting a table – indoors or out – can sometimes take a wait. But the food is terrific and the people-watching even better. After a cup of espresso at the News, begin the colorful stroll up Ocean Drive.

Just one block away on Ocean Drive is the Waldorf Towers, a yellow, purple and white Art Deco gem. Across the street is Volley-ball Beach, the place where young and beautiful beach bums hang-out to meet with friends and play volley ball. Along the same street you'll find the Café des Arts, an elegant pink apartment building with an excellent French restaurant on the first floor. At 10th Street is the Miami Beach Ocean Front Auditorium, a place where local people, both young and old, congregate for lectures, lunches and music.

A few blocks to the north at 10th Street and Ocean Drive is the **Art Deco Welcome Center** (daily 11am–9pm or later). The Wel-come Center is run by the Miami Design Preservation League, the civic organization largely responsible for the preservation of Miami Beach's Art Deco architecture. The center sells Art Deco antiques and jewelry, books and postcards, and is a good place to learn about the history of Art Deco. Saturday morning walking tours of the district depart from the gift shop.

The next block includes three more classic Art Deco hotels – the Carlyle, Cardozo, and Cavalier – that were among the first of the beach hotels to be restored. They are all spectacular structures and well-run hotels. To the east of Ocean Drive is Lummus Park, eight blocks of wide, white beach-front where kite-flyers, sunbathers, and joggers all jockey for space.

At the northern end of Ocean Drive just past the blue and white Betsy Ross Hotel, turn left at 15th Street, walk one block and you will be on the world-famous **Collins Avenue**. Although not as glamorous as you perhaps imagined it, Collins Avenue a little far-ther to the north is where the grand 1950s hotels like the Eden Roc and the Fontainebleau can be found.

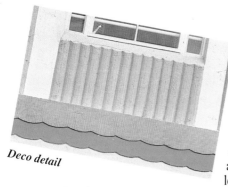
Deco detail

Walk one block north on Collins Avenue and you will come to the Lincoln Road Mall. At the corner of Lincoln Road and Collins is the world's only Art Deco Burger King. The greasy burger joint is housed in one of South Beach's classic pink and green Deco structures. Turn left and take a walk down Lincoln Road, a pedestrian-only street that was once one of Miami Beach's most up-scale shopping districts. During the past few years Lincoln Road has been part of the South Beach renaissance and many of the old shops have been turned into art galleries and fine restaurants. Although there are still plenty of junky little stores lining the street, Lincoln Road is heading toward recovery. It is home to the South Florida Art Center, a collective of over 100 local artists; the Lincoln Theater, home-base for Miami's New World Symphony; the Area Theater, a cozy and intimate playhouse; and the Miami City Ballet. At No 905 Lincoln Road, the ballet headquarters has a large window where locals come to watch the dancers warm up and practice their steps.

Along with Lincoln Road, two other streets worth exploring in South Beach are **Washington Avenue** and **Espanola Way**. Washington is one block west and parallel to Collins Avenue. It's a busy street full of delicatessens, second-hand shops, restaurants, fruit markets and bakeries. It's a very local experience where you will find elderly ladies bargaining with a butcher for a piece of meat and young roller-skaters on their way home from school. Espanola Way, one block west of Washington Avenue just south of 15th Street, is one of the prettiest streets on the beach. At the corner is the Miami Beach International Youth Hostel, also known as the Clay Hotel. The striking pink Mediterranean Revival building is where Cuban band leader Desi Arnaz made his American debut. Today the building houses a hostel popular with young,

Bar folk on Ocean Driv

European tourists. It continues down the rest of the street and in places is adorned with hand-painted tiles and balconies. It served as the backdrop for the popular television show *Miami Vice*.

Espanola Way also has a unique collection of vintage clothing outlets, antique jewelry stores and art boutiques for those with shopping on their minds.

The Art Deco District

11. Little Havana

While it doesn't have the grand boulevards or historic architecture of its namesake, Miami's neighborhood of Little Havana offers the most intense Cuban experience this side of the Gulf Stream. It makes for a lively afternoon excursion that will introduce you to a culture that is full of warmth, bravado and a zest for life.

Hand-rolling cigars

Located to the west of downtown, the heart of Little Havana lies along SW 8th Street, known in the neighborhood as **Calle Ocho**. A stroll down Calle Ocho will be enlivened by ethnic encounters, bursts of salsa music pouring on to the streets, and the smell of garlic wafting through the air. Calle Ocho is also where the annual 23-block long Cuban street festival – simply called Calle Ocho – takes place each March.

Starting at the eastern part of the street near 11th Avenue is the **El Credito Cigar Factory** (Monday to Saturday 8am–5pm). Founded in Cuba in 1907, El Credito is a working cigar factory that makes you feel like you're in Havana of 1950. Women and men sit around all day chopping tobacco and hand-rolling the potent-smelling cigars that made Cuba famous. Although few people in the shop speak English, visitors are welcome for a quick tour.

Nearby is the **Botanica la Abuela** (Monday to Saturday 10am–5pm), a Cuban-style pharmacy that sells religious paraphernalia for the Afro-Cuban religion of Santeria.

Domino demons on Calle Ocho

Near 13th Avenue and 8th Street is **La Casa de Los Trucos** (Monday to Saturday 10am–6pm), another Havana transplant and neighborhood institution that sells magic tricks, masks, costumes and silly toys for adults and children. Across the street is **Los Pinarenos** (Monday to Saturday 9am–5pm), an open-air Cuban market that specializes in tropical fruits and vegetables. At the western corner of 13th Avenue (also known as Cuban Memorial

Boulevard) and 8th Street is the **Bay of Pigs Monument**, a somber memorial that pays tribute to the Cuban men who lost their lives in the foiled invasion of Cuba in 1961. Schoolchildren often come to the monument to place flowers and say a prayer alongside the eternal flame.

At the corner of 8th Street and 15th Avenue is **Maximo Gomez Park**, more commonly known as Domino Park. In this little fenced-in park, elderly Cuban men gather for games of dominos. The Spanish-speaking, cigar-smoking gentlemen talk about the good-old-days in their native Cuba, and dream about the day when they can go back home. Although a park custom asks that only men over 55 enter the grounds, visitors, including women, are welcome.

Farther west on 8th Street, near 21st Avenue, is **Bellas Artes** (Tel: 305-325 0515), a Spanish-language theater house that specializes in Latin

Joking apart

productions. The plays, that range from classic dramas to comedies about the current hard times in Cuba, are usually an outrageous spectacle, and the audience is often as much fun as the performance.

Toward the western end of Little Havana's Calle Ocho at 32nd Avenue is the **Woodlawn Park Cemetery** (daily 10am–5pm). The peaceful, tree-lined grounds dotted with elaborate and well-maintained tombs are where many well-known Cubans are buried, including three former presidents of the island. Also buried here is Anastasio Somosa, the Nicaraguan dictator whose family operates several restaurants in Miami.

The last stop on 8th Street is for a home-style Cuban dinner at the **Versailles Restaurant** (daily 8am–2am) on 35th Avenue. A favorite among the established Cuban community, Versailles is a noisy and garish spot that has become a celebrated landmark in the neighborhood. Reasonably priced, the meals are filling and typical of the robust cooking Cuban grandmothers are famous for. Try the roast pork, fried bananas, and *arroz con pollo*.

53

12. Coconut Grove

A tour of Miami's vibrant Coconut Grove, with its shops, tropical architecture and wintering pop stars.

One of the oldest and lushest areas of Miami, Coconut Grove is a colorful neighborhood of funky houses with a spirited center of outdoor cafés, shops and galleries that hums with street life day and night. Once a mecca for artists and writers, the Grove has changed its character in recent years, leaning more toward the commercial than the bohemian, but it is still a place where Miamians love to spend their weekends.

Located a few miles south of downtown and east of US1, the center of Coconut Grove is best reached by driving east from US1 at the intersection of McDonald Street until you get to Grand Avenue. Public parking areas are scattered throughout the center district; most require coins for the meters. To the south of McDonald Street on Grand Avenue is the Bahamian neighborhood of the Grove. In the late 1800s many of the island residents settled in the area to help build the city. Their presence is still prominent and the neighborhood is full of small, island-style houses.

A place for free spirits

From McDonald Street northward to Mary Street, Grand Avenue is full of commercial activity. Near Virginia Street and Grand Avenue is **CocoWalk** (Sunday to Thursday 11am–10pm, Friday and Saturday 11am–midnight), a shopping area and entertainment center. The multi-level pink and white complex is full of chain stores and independent boutiques, bars, restaurants, and an eight-screen movie theater. The center courtyard, adorned with towering palm trees, often has live music at night and on weekends. Some of the more lively bars are on the upper levels: Tu Tu Tango, Baja Beach Club, and Hooters are all boisterous places that attract a young crowd. Also upstairs is the Improv Comedy Club, a sophisticated dinner club that features comedy acts.

Across the street from CocoWalk is **Mayfair in the Grove**, another shopping and restaurant complex with the plush 180-room Mayfair House hotel as the centerpiece. More sophisticated than CocoWalk, the Mayfair complex has over 50 very exclusive and very expensive shops. Although not the place to pick up a bargain, it is worth looking around. One of its more offbeat spots is the Oak Feed Store (daily 10am–9pm), a well-stocked health foods store and restaurant liked by New Age types. It is also home to **Planet Hollywood**, the movie memorabilia theme restaurant.

Back toward the south end of Grand Avenue is **Commodore Plaza**, a fashionable, one-block long street jam-packed with cafés and shops. On the south side of Commodore is the Grove Harbour Courtyard, a tri-level complex of shops and restaurants. Also in the complex is the Carlos Art Gallery (Monday to Saturday 11am–9pm, Sunday 11am–6pm), one of the best Haitian art galleries in the city. Next door on the second-floor is the Kaleidoscope, an elegant tropical restaurant with a first-class menu. The end of Commodore Plaza intersects with Main Highway, another busy street in the Grove. Both corners of the intersection are outdoor cafés which are favorite spots for people-watching.

A few blocks to the south on Main Highway is the Coconut Grove Playhouse, an intimate little theater built in 1926. Next door is the **Taurus**, a popular steak-house that attracts a professional happy-hour crowd on week-nights. Across the street from here, tucked away behind old banyan trees, is the **Barnacle State Historic Site** (Thursday to Sunday 9am–4pm). The former home of the Miami pioneer Commodore Ralph Munroe, the Barnacle is a perfectly preserved 100-year-old house furnished with period antiques, lace curtains and oriental rugs. Designed with a natural air-conditioning system of vents and fans, it is always refreshingly cool from the breezes that blow off Biscayne Bay, and is an amazing example of what life in Miami was like in its early days. The small entrance fee is well worth the price and includes a narrated tour of the house and grounds.

The north side of Main Highway is lined with ice-cream parlors, clothing and swimwear boutiques, and gift shops. It ends at the intersection of McFarlane Road which slopes down a hill toward **Peacock Park**, a waterfront playground that hosts festivals and concerts throughout the year. At the foot of McFarlane Road is South Bayshore Drive, a road that leads past the **Dinner Key Marina** where hundreds of sailboats and yachts are moored.

By continuing on South Bayshore Drive, a few miles to the north, you will reach the **Vizcaya Museum and Gardens** (daily 9.30am–5pm; gardens open till 5.30pm). Built between 1914 and 1916, Vizcaya is a 70-room Italian Renaissance-style palace that looks as if it is 300 years old. Over 10,000 laborers were employed in its construction which includes Cuban barrel tile roofs and wrought-iron grillwork. The former winter home of the American industrialist James Deering,

Vizcaya Museum

Vizcaya is filled with European antiques, art and tapestries. Its interior includes a banqueting hall, tea room and library.

The exterior grounds, about 10 acres of land, comprise manicured European gardens with decorative urns, statues and fountains and a series of islands connected by bridges. Although the gardens were badly damaged during Hurricane Andrew, the house was left unharmed. An outdoor café, nestled beside a coral rock grotto and swimming-pool, serves surprisingly good food and drinks. While Vizcaya attracts over 250,000 visitors a year and is one of Coconut Grove's greatest attractions, there's a house nearby that also attracts a lot of attention these days. On Brickell Avenue, just to the north of the Vizcaya grounds, is a bayfront Mediterranean mansion owned by Madonna. Although the pop star tries to keep a low profile while she winters in Coconut Grove, paparazzi often hide in the bushes outside her home just waiting for a chance to catch her frolicking in the sun.

13. The Everglades

A morning excursion to the Everglades National Park.

Although the charms of **Everglades National Park** are subtle – ripples on the water as an alligator passes, a mild flutter when an egret takes off, or a slight change in the color of the grass as the winds blow – the park continues to fascinate travelers from around the world with its vast wetlands.

Located about 25 miles west of Miami on the **Tamiami Trail** (8th Street), the Everglades makes a peaceful morning excursion from the city. Since the afternoons are awfully hot, and much of the wildlife activity takes place early in the morning, it's best to plan on reaching the park by 8am.

Don't forget to bring along a hat and sun-block lotion, and mosquito repellent if it's summer time. And although it's tempting, do not feed the alligators. They are wild creatures and have been known to bite off arms.

Mangrove country

Everglade emblem

Once you drive past the ugly shopping centers and suburban housing complexes, the Tamiami Trail becomes a quiet two-lane road surrounded by the fresh waters of the Everglades. A shallow, slow-moving river that looks like a field of wet grass, the Everglades is about 100 miles long and 50 miles wide and provides South Florida with most of its water.

Although severely damaged by Hurricane Andrew in 1992, the eco-system of the Everglades is resilient, and most ecologists say that the physical damage done to the plant and animal life – deer, otters, turtles, alligators, manatees and eagles – was just nature's way of cleaning out the old in preparation for the new.

There's not enough time to visit all of the spots on Tamiami Trail in one morning or even a whole day, so decide whether you'd rather mingle with Native Americans, walk amid nature, or take a thrilling airboat ride, and plan your morning accordingly.

The first choice on the Trail is **Coopertown's** (daily 8am–7pm). One of several outfits offering airboat rides in the Everglades, Coopertown's is perhaps the least commercial and most fun. For a reasonable price, a guide takes you out in a flat-bottom boat for an exciting and noisy 30-minute ride.

Just west of Coopertown's is **Everglades Safari Park** (daily 8.30am–5pm). Although a bit too popular with the tour-bus crowd, the Safari Park is a rustic complex with quiet nature trails, boat rides, a wildlife museum and craft shop.

Further along the Trail from the Safari Park is the entrance to **Shark Valley** (daily 8.30am–6pm, entrance fee). Part of Everglades National Park, Shark Valley is run by the National Parks Service and is one of the least commercial stops on the Trail. Located at the headwaters of the Shark River, it is a secluded spot with a helpful information center. A heavy, musky smell from the dense plant life hangs in the air. A 15-mile road loops through the park and can be explored by taking one of the narrated tram tours, renting a bicycle, or by walking. An observation tower inside the grounds offers a broad view of the surrounding wetlands.

About one mile past Shark Valley is the **Miccosukee Indian Village and Restaurant** (daily 9am–5pm, entrance fee). A real-life Indian reservation, the Miccosukee Village offers the chance to learn about the tribe through village tours. These include lessons on their language, life style, and craft-making. The gift shop sells moccasins, jewelry, pottery and the brightly colored patchwork clothing.

Even if you don't visit the reservation, the Miccosukee restaurant is the best place on the Trail to stop for lunch. With an airy view of the water, it serves traditional Indian foods like pumpkin and Indian fry bread, fried catfish, frogs' legs and gatortail. And after a sweaty morning, you'll want to wash it down with an ice-cold beer.

Key West

About 155 miles south of Miami (and 90 miles north of Havana), Key West can be reached from Miami either by a 40-minute flight, or a three-hour drive along the Florida Keys Overseas Highway (also known as US1). Mile-markers, posted on the side of the highway, begin with number 126 in Florida City south of Miami, and end with the zero marker in the heart of Key West. Although tourists who are pressed for time sometimes make a one-day trip to Key West, the city deserves at least a two-day stay to soak up the rich atmosphere and get a feel for what it's really about.

Duval Street, Key West

As the last of the 31 islands that make up the Florida Keys, and the southernmost city in the continental US, Key West is, and always has been, a refuge for characters who rebel against conformity and conservatism. It is an anything-goes kind of place where grandmothers selling fudge brownies from their bicycles, recent Cuban immigrants, and drag queens wearing sequined dresses live side-by-side. One of the more colorful cities in Florida, Key West is proud of its decadent and hedonistic style.

In the 1800s Key West was the richest per capita city in the US, full of sponge divers, cigar makers, and pirates. Its historic architecture is charming, a combination New England and Caribbean styles, with pastel-colored gingerbread verandas, widow's walks, and wrought-iron balconies. Although only 4 miles long and 1½ miles wide, it is crammed with treasures. Its resident population is a small 25,000, but over 1 million tourists visit it annually.

Key West's substantial gay population is largely responsible for the city's recent renaissance that included sprucing up many of the run-down buildings and turning them into restaurants, guest houses, and art galleries. The local gays have also added Fantasy Fest, a flamboyant costume-party street festival – part gay pride parade and part Halloween bash – to the list of the city's attractions. And the city still has a fair number of writers who call it home, although the days when Ernest Hemingway and Tennessee Williams were a part of the landscape are long gone.

Born-on-the-island locals like to call themselves conchs (pronounced konks, as in the large seashell with an edible muscle). Conch cruisers are what locals call fat-tired bicycles, the favorite mode of transportation on the island. And a few years ago the city – half-jokingly – decided it wanted to secede from the US and declared itself the Conch Republic island nation.

Although Key West is best explored by bike or on foot, one of the easiest ways to get acquainted with the town before venturing out on your own is to take one of the **Conch Tour Train** rides (frequent departures daily 9am–4.30pm at either Mallory Square or Roosevelt Avenue). A Key West attraction since 1958, the Conch Train is a series of open-air carts pulled by an imitation locomotive train that rattles through the city for 90 minutes while the conductor points out spots of interest and explains the island's history.

The area known as **Old Town**, in the western portion of the island, is where you'll find most of Key West's great architecture and attractions. Two parallel streets in particular – Whitehead and Duval – lend themselves to leisurely walking tours. Depending upon how many stops you make, a stroll down one and then back up the other can take between five or six hours, leaving plenty of time to make it to Mallory Square for sunset.

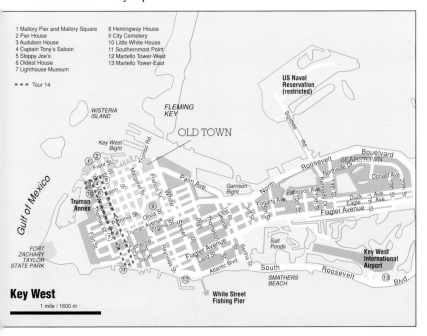

14. Whitehead and the Waterfront

A day exploring the Old Town and its maritime, literary, ethnic and practical heritage, adjourning to Sloppy Joe's for lunch. Evening of live entertainment on Mallory Square. It won't be possible to see all the museums mentioned here before lunch, so I suggest you pick and choose according to taste.

The best place to begin a day's walking tour is on the waterfront on the western edge of Old Town. On Greene Street, about two blocks from Whitehead Street, is the **Mel Fisher Maritime Heritage Society Museum** (daily 9.30am–5.30pm). Mel Fisher was a marine salvager who spent decades searching for sunken treasures off the waters of Key West. In the mid-1980s he amazed the world

Local produce

by finding a bounty of gold and silver bars, chains, coins, and jewels valued at about $4 billion from the Spanish galleons, the *Atocha* and the *Santa Margarita*, that sank in 1622. Fisher, who wore red suspenders and a huge gold medallion until his recent death, used to sit in the office at the rear of the museum, though he was more than willing to come out and meet visitors who asked for him. He'd even allow you to borrow his gold medallion necklace to take a photograph. The museum's small entrance fee entitles you to view the artifacts from the ships, including a beautiful 77-carat emerald, and learn about the marine salvage industry.

On the water at the end of Greene Street, near the intersection of Whitehead Street, is the **Little White House Museum** (daily 9am–5pm). Part of the **Truman Annex** complex, the Little White House, built in 1890, was the winter vacation home of President Harry S Truman. While president in the 1940s, Truman came here to swim, rest, drink bourbon, and play poker. The museum offers a guided house tour and a video chronicling the Truman era.

One block from Greene Street over on to the foot of Whitehead Street is the **Key West Aquarium** (daily 10am–6pm). For a small admission charge, the aquarium offers a vast selection of marine specimens from both the Gulf waters and the Atlantic Ocean and a touch tank that allows you to dip your hand into a pool of starfish, hermit crabs and horse conchs. About a block away, also on Whitehead Street, is the **Audubon House and Gardens** (daily 9.30am–5pm), an antique-filled, three-story home built in the mid-1840s in honor of the famed American ornithologist James John Audubon.

Hemingway's house

Ironically, Mr Audubon, for whom the Audubon Society conservation group was named, loved to hunt and kill birds and animals himself, and actually never set foot in this house, which is one of the island's architectural gems.

Further down on Whitehead Street, about six short blocks from the Audubon House, is a magnificent coral rock mansion with a wrought-iron second-story balcony. The **Hemingway House** (daily 9am–5pm) is one of the city's most popular attractions and is always full of tourists. It was here that Ernest Hemingway wrote *Death in the Afternoon*, *To Have and Have Not*, and *The Snows of Kilimanjaro*. The Nobel Prize-winning author lived here in the 1930s with his wife Pauline, their two sons, a nurse and a cook. For a small entrance fee, you can take a 30-minute narrated tour and see his writing study, hunting trophies, eclectic antique collection, and a variety of six-toed cats – descendants of Hemingway's personal menagerie. Occasionally, kittens are available for adoption, but there's a five-year waiting-list of devoted Hemingway fans. The swimming-pool in the courtyard was supposedly Key West's first.

Down the block and across the street from the Hemingway House is the **Lighthouse Museum** (daily 9.30am–5pm). Built in 1847, the 92-ft high lighthouse and adjacent keeper's home are now a museum filled with nautical charts, antique photographs, and lighthouse paraphernalia. A climb up the 98 lighthouse steps, although exhausting, gives you a panoramic view of the island.

After walking about six more blocks on Whitehead Street toward the dead-end water's edge, you will see a massive concrete marker, shaped like a buoy with red, black and yellow bands around it. This is the **Southernmost Point** in the continental US. While the marker itself is not much to look at, hundreds of tourists a day pose in front of it for photographs.

Parallel to and one block away from Whitehead is **Duval Street**, the main commercial thoroughfare and the liveliest street in the city. A one-mile long strip of bars, guest houses, restaurants, ice-cream parlors, art galleries and gift shops, Duval is a non-stop circus anytime of the day or night. As you follow Duval, you will be heading back to where you started.

In the 500 block of Duval, one of the first spots to visit is the **San**

The San Carlos Institute

Carlos Institute (Tuesday to Sunday 11am–5pm), a Cuban heritage museum, theater and cultural center. Founded in 1871, the Institute focuses on the contribution that Cuban exiles have made to Key West and is housed in a beautifully restored historic building. Take a close look at the hand-painted tiles that Cuban craftsmen are known for. There is a small admission fee.

Also on this block is the **Strand Theater**, an elaborately designed movie house built by Cuban craftsmen in 1918. Today, the Strand with its ornately decorated facade serves as home to the **Ripley's Believe It Or Not Museum** (daily 9am–11pm), a so-called 'odditorium' with displays that include shrunken heads, a hurricane wind tunnel, and antique diving gear. Across the street from the Strand is one of Key West's too-touristy-to-be-real attractions – the **Margaritaville Café** (daily 11am–4am). Here, owner Jimmy Buffet, the folk music hero and part-time Key West resident, has created a shrine to himself and his music. The café offers frosty margaritas and sells Jimmy Buffet souvenirs including records, books and Margaritaville underwear. If you are a diehard Buffet fan, you might want to stop here for one of the 'Cheeseburger in Paradise' lunches. Otherwise save yourself for lunch at Sloppy Joe's later (see below).

One block away from the Margaritaville Café is the stately **St Paul's Episcopal Church**. Damaged by three hurricanes, St Paul's was rebuilt with sturdy masonry work in 1919. Continuing on to the 300 block of Duval Street is the **Wreckers Museum** (Monday to Saturday 10am–4pm, Sunday noon–4pm) occupying the oldest house in Key West. Eighteenth-century antiques and historic photographs record the days when Key West pirates raided the ships supposedly 'wrecked' offshore and brought their booty to town.

Toward the end of Duval are two of the most-talked about spots in Key West. **Sloppy Joe's** (daily 9am–4am) at the corner of Duval and Green Streets, claims to have been Hemingway's favorite drinking hole. A boisterous and loud, good-time bar with Hemingway memorabilia and peanut shells on the floor, Sloppy Joe's is a great place for a late lunch of fish sandwiches and conch chowder. The bar, however, has been at this location only since the late 1930s; before that, the 'real' Sloppy Joe's where Hemingway actually did his drinking was a block away on Green Street at a place that is now called **Captain Tony's Saloon** (daily 10am–4am). Owned for decades by Tony Tarracino, a former gambler, bootlegger, and boat captain, Captain Tony's is the oldest bar in Key West. Built in 1852, the structure once served as the city morgue. Dark, dank and outlandish, the bar hasn't changed much in 50 years. Tarracino sold the bar in 1988 and a year later was elected mayor of Key West. Although he was good at cutting through bureaucratic nonsense, Tarracino had a vulgar, saloon-owner style that did not sit well

Modern-day pirate

Sunset on Mallory Pier

with many of the town's conservative residents and he was not re-elected. Both Captain Tony's and Sloppy Joe's make for a great way to pass a Key West afternoon.

When the end of the day rolls around, it's time to head over to Key West's most treasured happening – the sunset celebration. At the foot of Duval, on the waterfront, is where you will find **Mallory Square.** A cruise ship pier and public park, Mallory Square erupts each evening into a free-spirited party reminiscent of the 1960s hippie era. Starting at about half an hour before dusk, thousands of people congregate to watch the sun sink into the Gulf, and the collection of street performers who entertain the crowds. Some of the square's more creative acts include a fire-eating sword-swallower, a Harry Houdini-like man who ties himself up in chains and then laboriously wiggles free, and a cat-tamer who has trained ordinary domestic cats to jump safely through flaming hoops. There's always an array of live music entertainment along with fortune tellers, jugglers and clowns.

15. Around the Island

In addition to Duval and Whitehead Streets, there are a few other spots on the island worth seeking out. One of them is the several block area in Old Town known as **Bahama Village** on the southwest side of Whitehead Street. In the 1700s, many workers from the nearby Bahama Islands settled in Key West to help build the city. Their knowledge of tropical architecture and foliage is one of the reasons Key West has such a Caribbean feel to it. Much of the city's substantial Bahamian population still lives in this neigh-

Bahama Village mural

Off to school in Bahama Village

borhood. Throughout Bahama Village, wooden houses, painted bright pinks, blues, and greens, dot the streets, and small grocery stores selling Bahamian specialties bustle with activity. One of the most popular places is **Blue Heaven** (Wednesday to Sunday 8am–3pm and 6–10pm) at the corner of Thomas and Petronia Streets. Housed in a three-story Greek Revival clapboard structure, Blue Heaven is a very casual Bahamian/Caribbean restaurant that serves curried fish and conch. In former days, the building served as a bordello, boxing and cock-fighting arena. One corner of the property still contains a rooster graveyard.

On the other side of Old Town, in a dense residential neighborhood, is the **Tennessee Williams Home**. The modest, white frame house with tomato-red shutters, is located on Duncan Street near the corner of Leon Street. Not open to the public, the house is now a private residence. The Pulitzer Prize-winning playwright, best known for his works *A Streetcar Named Desire*, *The Glass Menagerie*, and *Night of the Iguana*, lived and wrote here for 34 years before his death in 1983.

About 10 blocks away from the Tennessee Williams Home on Angela Street is the **Key West Cemetery**. Established in 1847, the cemetery is crowded with above-the-ground vaults with frangipani, sausage, and palm trees providing shade.

Many of the tombs have inscriptions that are as irreverent as Key West itself. Among them: *I Told You I Was Sick*, *The Buck Stops Here*, and *Here Lies My Heart*. One of the tombs holds the remains of Elena Hoyos Mesa, a beautiful Cuban woman who was the object of a mad obsession by a Key West man named Karl von Cosel. When the woman died in the 1930s, Cosel dug up her corpse, covered it with wax, dressed it in a wedding gown, and kept it in his home for seven years before the authorities discovered the grisly scene and returned the body to its tomb.

16. A Day at the Beach

Although better known for its architecture and offbeat character, Key West has beautiful public beaches along the southern side of the island. Even though they're often covered with seaweed and chunks of coral, and the waters offshore are too shallow for serious swimming, the beaches satisfy a bake-in-the-sun desire, and are worth devoting a day to after you've explored the city. Most are open from sunrise to sunset and only charge a fee for parking. Since many locals squeeze in a day at the beach as part of their weekly schedule, they are often crowded. Don't forget to pack a big towel and sun-block lotion. And although most of the beaches have food and drink vendors nearby, a lunch packed in town beforehand will usually be more satisfying.

At the foot of White Street is the **White Street Pier**, a popular fishing and sunbathing spot. Facing the pier, to the left along South Roosevelt Boulevard, is **Smathers Beach**, the longest beach on the island. Smathers is usually packed with beautiful young windsurfers, bathers, and kite-flyers. In the distance, about a mile away from Smathers Beach near the Key West Airport, you can spot the **East Martello Tower** (daily 9.30am–5pm), a huge, brick Civil War fort that houses an art and history museum run by the **Key West Art and Historical Society**. On your way home from the beach you might want to stop at the museum to see the displays on pirating, sponging, turtling, local artists and writers.

A game bird

On the right side of the White Street Pier is **Higgs Beach**, the second largest beach on the island. With picnic tables and a playground, Higgs Beach attracts families with small children. A thick grove of Australian Pine trees provides respite from the sun.

At the end of Vernon and Waddell Streets is a small, public beach which allows topless bathing and dogs. **Fort Zachary Taylor State Historic Site**, near the Truman Annex at the western end of the island, is a quiet family beach with picnic tables and barbecue grills.

Shopping

Although not thought to be the stuff trea-sure-hunters' dreams are made of, Florida does offer shoppers an array of affordable goodies to take home from a trip. Aside from the tacky tourist traps – of which there are thousands – where rub-ber alligators, Mickey Mouse ears and orange perfume comprise the bulk of the stock, there are stores selling designer clothing at fac-tory prices, primitive Caribbean art, and sand-polished shells that forever smell of the sea. Surprisingly, Florida is a good place for antiques because of the many transplanted retirees who hauled their life's belongings with them. Estate sales, advertised in local newspapers, are often a collector's delight. In addition, many antique dealers from around the country set up shop in Florida dfuring the winter months. Hours may vary, but most shopping centers are open seven days a week.

Plenty in store

Orlando

The **Belz Factory Outlet Mall** (Mon-day to Saturday 10am–9pm, Sunday 10am–6pm; 5401 West Oakridge Road at the northern end of International Drive, Tel: 407-352 9600), the second most-visited 'attraction' in Orlando after Disney World, is a bargain bonanza. This large, indoor mall is made up of four buildings that house almost 100 stores. Belz is the best place in Florida to shop for designer clothes – Anne Klein, London Fog, Christian Dior and many more – and just about ev-ery brand of blue jeans, sneakers and casual wear at discounts of up to 75 percent off retail prices.

Flea World (Friday to Sunday 9am–6pm, Highway 17–92 just north of Orlando, Tel: 407-321 1792) calls itself America's largest flea market, and with 1,000 dealers spreading their wares over 100 acres of land, it may well be. With garage-sale clean outs, dis-counted merchandise, and Florida antiques, Flea World is a fa-vorite weekend diversion.

Florida's most famous fruit

The sweet and juicy citrus fruits grown in the center of the state are known worldwide, so stop at **Orange World** – everything in the Orlando area seems to be a 'world' of some sort or another – (daily 8am–11pm, 5395 West Irlo Bronson Memorial Highway, Kissimmee, Tel: 407-396 1306) for a squeeze-while-you-wait drink. You can't miss the building – shaped like a gigantic orange – and inside is an assortment of fresh-picked fruits, citrus candies and orange blossom honey, all available to be shipped to your friends and family back home.

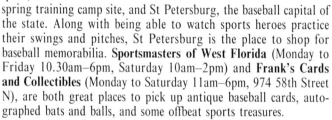

Tampa/St Petersburg

Baseball, America's most-watched sport, has made Florida its favorite spring training camp site, and St Petersburg, the baseball capital of the state. Along with being able to watch sports heroes practice their swings and pitches, St Petersburg is the place to shop for baseball memorabilia. **Sportsmasters of West Florida** (Monday to Friday 10.30am–6pm, Saturday 10am–2pm) and **Frank's Cards and Collectibles** (Monday to Saturday 11am–6pm, 974 58th Street N), are both great places to pick up antique baseball cards, autographed bats and balls, and some offbeat sports treasures.

A good spot for antique hunting in Tampa is the **Interbay Antique Row** (MacDill and El Prado Avenues near Bayshore Boulevard). It's a shopper's paradise, with dozens of stores spread throughout the area selling all kinds of antique furniture, old postcards, art, Art Deco jewelry and vintage clothing.

Miami

For up-scale shopping, one of Miami's most elegant centers is the **Bal Harbour Shops** (Monday to Saturday 10am–9pm, Sunday noon–6pm; 9700 Collins Avenue, Bal Harbour, Tel: 305-866 0311) at the northern end of Miami Beach. The beautiful and elegant center houses Neiman Marcus, Gucci, Fendi, and Ann Taylor boutiques, and offers fine al fresco dining.

If you're after a bargain, it's worth a trip out of Miami to nearby Opa-Locka, site of one of the largest flea markets in South Florida. At the **Opa-Locka/Hialeah Flea Market** (daily 5am–7pm; free parking Monday through

Goods out of Africa

Friday), more than 1,200 wholesale and retail vendors showcase their stuff. There are also more than a dozen restaurants featuring international cuisine and beer. The flea market draws large crowds year-round; selling everything from dolls to dishes, it's the place to check out for anyone working on a hobby or collection.

Key West

Along with drinking silly rum concoctions with paper umbrellas in them, shopping is one of the most popular pastimes in Key West. While everyone agrees that in recent years the town has become cluttered with far too many T-shirt shops, Key West also has a funky collection of art galleries, shell boutiques and jewelry stores. **Key West Aloe** (daily 9am–8pm, 524 Front Street, Tel: 305-294 5592) produces hundreds of perfumes, sunscreens and skin care products from the native aloe plant. Their products are all natural and refreshing, and aloe gel is one of the best remedies for sunburn. The company's factory, a few blocks from the shop, is open to the public for tours.

At **Key West Hand Print Fabrics** (daily 10am–6pm, 201 Simonton Street, Tel: 305-294 9535) workers make brightly colored, hand-printed cotton and silk fabrics that are sold by the yard and as casual clothing. **Fast Buck Freddie's** (daily 10am–6pm, 500 Duval Street, Tel: 305-294 2007), a Key West institution, is a department store that specializes in the bizarre – sequined bikinis, battery-operated alligators that bite, and fish-shaped shoes. The **Haitian Art Company** (daily 10am–6pm, 600 Frances Street, Tel: 305-296 8932) has one of the largest collections of paintings, sculptures, steel and papier-mâché art imported from Haiti in the US, and the **Gingerbread Square Gallery** (daily 11am–6pm, 901 Duval Street, Tel: 305-296 8900), the oldest gallery in Key West, features nationally prominent Key West artists.

Art for sale on Mallory Pier

Eating Out

In recent years, a new wave of cooking has surged through Florida's restaurants, using local tropical ingredients in all sorts of *nouvelle* styles. Coconut, citrus, mangoes, and green bananas combine with fresh, native seafood – grouper, snapper, pompano, conch, oysters, lobster, shrimp and crab.

A chef sets to work

Many of the immigrants who have settled in the state from Cuba, Jamaica, Peru, Nicaragua, Thailand, and Vietnam in the past 15 years have carved out a niche in the restaurant scene and their ethnic specialties are now a part of the Florida dining experience. And Florida, one of the largest cattle producing states in the country, is a sure bet for a good steak or juicy prime rib dinner.

Old-fashioned Florida dining, the kind that existed before mass tourism became the norm, can still be found at small, mom-and-pop cafés in inland areas, and usually means fried catfish and cornmeal hush puppies, grilled alligator tail, frogs' legs, heart of palm salad, and Seminole Indian fried bread. For big eaters on a budget, Florida is the land of the Early Bird Special, a three-course meal usually offered at a reduced price between the hours of 4–6pm, when a restaurant would otherwise be quiet. Sunday buffet brunches, and all-you-can-eat specials are also popular.

Price categories listed below are based on the average cost of a three-course meal without drinks. $ = under $15, $$ = $15–25, $$$ = over $25. Gratuities are usually not added on to the bill. The best domestic wines usually come from California or New York, and range in price between $10 and $50 per bottle.

Catch of the day

Orlando

MEL'S AMERICAN GRAFFITI DRIVE-IN
*1000 Universal Studios Plaza
Universal Studios, Orlando
Tel: 407-363 8766*
One of the better theme restaurants at the edge of the Universal Studios, with heavy emphasis on '50s decor and food. $

LE COQ AU VIN
*4800 South Orange Avenue, Orlando
Tel: 407-851 6980*
Considered the finest French restaurant in central Florida. Specialties include rainbow trout with champagne, roast duckling, and chicken liver pâté. $$$

BARNEY'S STEAK & SEAFOOD
*1615 East Colonial Drive
Orlando
Tel: 407-896-6864*
In addition to its enormous salad bar, Barney's offers prime cuts of beef and seafood creations in a family-style atmosphere. $$

POWER HOUSE
*111 East Lyman Avenue
Winter Park*
Tel: 407-645 3616
Inexpensive and healthy food with a 1960s feel and taste, a half-block from trendy Winter Park's Park Avenue. The herb tea and sandwiches are excellent. $

FORT LIBERTY
*5260 West Irlo Bronson Memorial
Boulevard, Kissimmee
Tel: 407-351 5151
(Ask for restaurant)*
A Wild West, cowboys and Indians dinner show restaurant. The food is all-American (typical fare is fried chicken and corn-on-the-cob), as is the shoot-'em-dead floor show. Make reservations. $$$

Tampa/St Petersburg

SKIPPERS SMOKE HOUSE
*910 Skipper Road
Tampa
Tel: 813-971 0666*
Florida and Caribbean specialties like curried chicken, smoked oysters, gatortail and shark in a rustic setting surrounded by oak trees. $$

BERN'S STEAK HOUSE
*1208 South Howard Avenue
Tampa*

Cupcakes to go

Tel: 813-251 2421
Bern's offers prime cuts of beef, organic vegetables, and over 7,000 bottles of wine to choose from. Reservations recommended. *$$$*

LEVEROCK'S SEAFOOD HOUSE
10 Corey Avenue
St Pete Beach
Tel: 727-367 4588
Inexpensive and casual seafood dining. A local favorite. *$*

OUTBACK STEAKHOUSE
4088 Park Street North
St Petersburg
Tel: 727-384 4329
Grilled shrimp and massive steaks served with a Down Under Australian attitude. *$$*

COLUMBIA RESTAURANT
2117 East 7th Avenue
Ybor City
Tel: 813-248 4961
In business since way back in 1905, the Columbia Restaurant specializes in fine Spanish foods complete with a flamenco dance show in the background for fun. *$$*

CRAWDADDY'S
2500 Rocky Point Drive
Tampa
Tel: 813-281 0407
A favorite locals' hangout that serves up gatortail and French fries. Has a funky atmosphere. *$*

Miami

PUERTO SAGUA
700 Collins Avenue
Miami Beach
Tel: 305-673 1115
Noisy and crowded with plenty of character. Puerto Sagua serves some of the heartiest Cuban food to be found in Miami. *$*

P F CHANG'S
8888 SW 136th Street
Miami
Tel: 305-2342338
Popular but pricey restaurant serving lunch and dinner only and promising traditional Chinese food with American hospitality. *$$*

SNAPPER'S RESTAURANT
Bayside Marketplace
Miami
Tel: 305-379 0605
Fresh seafood with a waterfront view. Emphasis on stone crabs, steaks, pasta and casual dining. *$$*

SOUTHFORK CAFE
3301 Rickenbacker Causeway
Key Biscayne
Tel: 305-365 9391

Dinner at Versailles

Located in a downtown marina, with Tex-Mex specialties, indoor or outdoor dining and live Caribbean music. Dock your boat free, too. *$$*

LOS RANCHOS
401 Biscayne Boulevard
Miami
Tel: 305-375 8188
Terrific Nicaraguan specials for hungry compadres in downtown's Bayside Marketplace. *$$*

SUNDAYS ON THE BAY
5420 Crandon Boulevard

Roadside stalls are hard to resist

Key Biscayne
Tel: 305-361 6777
Best place in Miami for a bayfront view and a grand, Sunday buffet brunch. $$

VERSAILLES RESTAURANT
3555 SW 8th Street
Miami

Espresso expert

Tel: 305-444 0240
This gem is a landmark restaurant located in Little Havana, where you'll be served typical Cuban cuisine. For a recommended specialty try the delicious roast pork which is served with fried bananas. $

Key West

LOUIE'S BACKYARD
700 Waddell Avenue
Tel: 305-294 1061
Fine American and Caribbean cooking served in a romantic, seaside setting. Old Key West ambience. $$$

A & B LOBSTER HOUSE
700 Front Street
Tel: 305-294 5880
Casual seafood dining with a beautiful harbor view. $$

SUNSET PIER
Zero Duval Street
Tel: 305-296 7701
A pleasantly relaxed, T-shirts and sandals kind of place which offers conch fritters, smoked fish, and frosty bottled beers. $

CAFÉ DES ARTISTES
1007 Simonton Street
Tel: 305-294 7100
An intimate and elegant setting noted for its classic French/tropical specialties like lobster in cognac sauce and shrimp in mango butter. Reservations required. $$$

Nightlife

Although the plentiful sunlight is what draws most travelers to Florida, the state is not lacking in big city, bright-light entertainment. Nightlife activities are abundant and the choice spreads across a wide range: romantic dinner cruises, Broadway plays, reggae bars, comedy clubs, classical ballet, flamenco shows, beach parties, gay discos, symphony orchestras, and open-air saloons.

In fall and winter months, nationally prominent entertainers make their way south and big-name acts can be found in most of Florida's large cities. Calypso kings and salsa queens from the Caribbean also tend to visit the state then, and local orchestra, theater and dance troupes perform.

Throughout the year, you will find plenty of nightclubs to satisfy night-owl cravings for music and dancing till the early-morning hours. On the wilder, crazier, exhibitionist side there are a number of bars offering ladies' wet T-shirt contests and karaoke nights.

Attire for most evening happenings, except for classical music concerts, dance performances or the theater, is usually very casual. The legal drinking age in Florida is 21 and identification is required.

Miami: bright lights, big city

Orlando

CARR PERFORMING ARTS CENTER
401 Livingston Street, Orlando
Tel: 407-849 2070
A year-round community auditorium that hosts regional and national music, theater and dance troupes.

ORLANDO ARENA
600 West Amelia Street
Tel: 407-849 2070
One of the main entertainment venues for evening events and concerts in the Orlando area.

RIVERSHIP ROMANCE
433 North Palmetto, Sanford
Tel: 407-321 5091
North of Orlando about 15 miles near I-4. The Rivership Romance is a southern-style paddlewheel ship that offers dinner and dancing cruises along the St John's River. Reservations required.

Close encounters

HARD ROCK CAFÉ ORLANDO
5401 South Kirkman Road, Orlando
Tel: 407-351-ROCK
The international chain has brought its rock-and-roll formula to Florida and the young people love it.

PLEASURE ISLAND
Disney Village, Lake Buena Vista
Tel: 407-934 7781
This 6-acre complex of nighttime entertainment includes seven nightclubs, movie theaters, restaurants, a comedy club, and a rock-and-roll beach club.

PHINEAS PHOGG'S BALLOON WORKS
129 West Church Street, Orlando
Tel: 407-422 2434
A popular, pulsating disco that draws tourists as well as locals.

HOOP-DEE-DOO REVUE
Disney Village, Lake Buena Vista
Tel: 407-934 7639
A corny, but lively, family show full of singing, dancing and clowning around.

Tampa/St Petersburg

STARLITE PRINCESS
3400 Pasadena Avenue South,
St Petersburg
Tel: 727-367 7804
Dinner and dancing cruises along the Intracoastal Waterway aboard a triple-deck ship.

TAMPA THEATER
711 Franklin Street, Tampa
Tel: 813-274 8981
This is a restored 1926 movie palace offering concerts, foreign films and special events.

TAMPA BAY PERFORMING ARTS CENTER
1010 North MacInnes Place, Tampa
Tel: 813-222 1000
One of the largest performing arts centers to be found in Florida. The three theaters host a variety of classical and popular entertainment.

JOYLAND COUNTRY NIGHT CLUB
11225 US19, St Petersburg
Tel: 727-573 1919
A Country & Western music and dance club. Cowboy boots suggested.

A visiting dance company

COLISEUM BALLROOM
534 4th Avenue North
St Petersburg
Tel: 727-892 5202
Late-night popular music dance club that occasionally features old-fashioned ballroom dancing.

CHA CHA COCONUTS
City Pier
St Petersburg
Tel: 727-822 6655
Live jazz concerts with a spectacular view of the water.

FLORIDA WEST COAST SYMPHONY
Tel: 727-953 4252
A regional orchestra that performs at several area venues.

RUTH ECKERD HALL
1111 McCullen Booth Road
Clearwater
Tel: 727-791-7400
Just north of St Petersburg, this venue hosts all types of musical events from rock to symphony concerts all year round.

Miami

MIAMI CITY BALLET
Tel: 305-532 4800
Miami City Ballet is a Latin-flavored classical ballet company with hints of jazz and modern dance. Various Miami locations.

NEW WORLD SYMPHONY
Tel: 305-673 3330
A first-rate repertoire of classical music performed at various theaters and occasionally in the city's moonlit, waterfront parks.

JACKIE GLEASON THEATER OF THE PERFORMING ARTS
1700 Washington Avenue,
Miami Beach

Tel: 305-673 7300
Ultra-modern theater hosting Broadway plays September through May.

COLONY THEATER
1040 Lincoln Road
Miami Beach
Tel: 305-674 1026
This former movie house turned cozy theater in the Art Deco District hosts offbeat music and stage performances.

TOBACCO ROAD
626 South Miami Avenue
Miami
Tel: 305-374 1198
A great old, smoke-filled saloon with live late-night jazz and blues bands.

BACCHANALLIA
1450 Collins Avenue
Miami Beach
Tel: 305-531 4499
A place-to-be-seen gay dance club for those who like to play at dressing up.

CENTRO VASCO
2235 SW 8th Street
Little Havana
Tel: 305-643-9606
The place to find the hottest Cuban performers this side of Havana.

LES VIOLINS
1751 Biscayne Boulevard
Miami
Tel: 305-371 8668
A flashback to Havana 1955, this late-night dinner club puts on a se-

quin and feathers floor show with lots of Latin flamboyance.

Key West

TENNESSEE WILLIAMS FINE ARTS CENTER
5901 Junior College Road
Tel: 305-296 1520
A 490-seat theater that presents plays, dance, classical and jazz concerts year-round.

WATERFRONT PLAYHOUSE
Mallory Square
Tel: 305-294 5015
This 1800s salvage warehouse now hosts comedy and dramatic acts November through May.

CELEBRITIES
430 Duval Street
Tel: 305-296 4600
Housed in La Concha Holiday Inn, this piano bar is popular with locals and is easy to find.

HAVANA DOCKS LOUNGE
1 Duval Street
Tel: 305-296 4600

A second-floor waterfront disco where locals and tourists come to dance the night away and watch the fish under the harbor lights.

THE GREEN PARROT
400 Southard Street
Tel: 305-294 6133
A well-known hangout with pool tables and dart boards; a bit raunchy but full of local color.

THE CHART ROOM
1 Duval Street
The Pier House Hotel
Tel: 305-296 4600
Dark and atmospheric and a tad expensive, the Chart Room is a popular gathering place for sophisticated late-night locals.

SLOPPY JOE'S BAR
Corner of Duval and Green Streets
Tel: 305-294 5717
One of the best-known night spots in Key West, Sloppy Joe's claims – somewhat dubiously – to have been Hemingway's hang-out. This boisterous good-time bar is decorated with Hemingway memorabilia.

The famous Sloppy Joe's

Calendar of Special Events

Since outdoor escapades are a way of life year-round in Florida, festivals are an expected phenomenon. Most take place in the winter months when the weather beckons everyone outside, but a few sweat-producing street fairs happen in the summer when out-of-town visitors, not accustomed to the tropics, can test their sun-and-fun endurance. Hundreds of special events go on throughout the year, ranging from re-enactments of black-bearded pirate raids to Latin dance parties that loosen up even the most rigid of spines. The following are some of Florida's most popular happenings.

JANUARY – FEBRUARY

The **Festival of the Epiphany** on January 6 is the Greek Orthodox Church's celebration of Christ's baptism. Just north of Tampa, the city of Tarpon Springs, Florida's largest Greek community (many of whom are transplanted sponge divers from the Greek islands), hosts an annual festival for the occasion (Tel: 727-937 3540). The **Art Deco Weekend** in mid-January is when the cotton-candy architecture of South Miami Beach attracts Deco-lovers from around the country for a weekend of sidewalk art

shows, 1920s big-band music and dancing under the stars (Tel: 305-672 2014).

In February, Tampa holds the **Gasparilla Festival**, a month-long party of parades, music and dramatizations about a pirate named José Gaspar, a nasty scoundrel who once terrorized ship captains as they sailed through Tampa Bay (Tel: 813-223 1111). The **Florida State Fair**, also in Tampa, takes place over the first two weeks in February. This all-American event includes carnival rides, country music, livestock shows, and county competitions. Mid-February brings two major events to Miami. The **Miami Film Festival**, a 10-day celebration of foreign, American and Florida films at venues throughout the city, attracts actors, directors and movie-buffs (Tel: 305-539 3000). The **Coconut Grove Arts Festival**, the state's largest, spills on to the streets with a backdrop of live music and the calming waters of Biscayne Bay (Tel: 305-447 0401).

MARCH – MAY

Early March means **Carnaval Miami**. The country's largest Hispanic festival that draws salsa- and mambo-lovers from around the Americas. Over a million people turn out for a week-long celebration of Latin music, dance and foods which culminates with a 23-block long street party in the heart of Miami's Little Havana neighborhood (Tel: 305-644 8888). During the **Conch Republic Celebrations**, late April and early May, independent-minded Key West honors its founding fathers and reminds the rest of Florida that it would rather be known as the 'Island Nation of Key West' (Tel: 305-294 4440).

JUNE – JULY

The **Miami/Bahamas Goombay Festival**, the first weekend in June, is heralded as the largest black heritage street fair in America. It is worth enduring the intense summer heat to attend. The Bahamian community of Coconut Grove puts on an island-style bash with Caribbean music, spicy seafood, and mighty potent rum. Originally linked to the freeing of the slaves in the Bahamas, the Goombay celebrations are known for their costumed 'Junkanoo' characters and raucous good-times (Tel: 305-372 9966).

The **Hemingway Days Festival** in mid-July is Key West's tribute to its favorite adopted son. The week-long party includes a literary conference, short-story competitions, a Papa Hemingway look-alike contest, and plenty of premeditated machismo madness (Tel: 305-294 4440).

OCTOBER – DECEMBER

Fantasy Fest in late October is Key West at its zaniest. The week-long bacchanalian bash starts with mask-making workshops and costume competitions, and ends with a twilight parade on Halloween night. There's even a pet masquerade contest (Tel:

305-294 4440)). **Light Up Orlando**, the second Saturday in November, is when downtown Orlando shows its theme-park neighbors that it too has something to ogle at. The city hosts an evening party with country music, fireworks, ethnic foods and roaming clowns (Tel: 407-648 4010).

During the December holiday season, waterways throughout Florida are aglow with twinkling lights as evening boat parades with Santas waving from the decks bring on the Yuletide spirit. Christmas in Florida – though lacking in snow – is joyous. Churches open their doors to tourists for services, as do synagogues during Chanukah. And celebrations on New Year's Eve are everywhere. One of the grandest is Miami's **King Orange Jamboree Parade** (Tel: 305-539 3063). The nationally televised spectacle of glitter and pomp ushers in the New Year with a celebrity line-up that snakes its way through downtown Miami. Millions of Americans tune in for the show.

The Goombay Festival, Miami

Practical Information

GETTING THERE

Over 40 million travelers a year journey to Florida, making it one of the most visited areas of the US. Many Americans consider a Florida vacation a birthright, and most make the pilgrimage to the Sunshine State at least once in their lives. In recent years international travelers – from Europe, South America and Japan – have also added Florida to their list of must-see places.

By Air

Most air travelers arrive at one of the state's three largest airports: Orlando International Airport, Tel: 407-825 2000; Tampa International Airport, Tel: 813-870 8700; and Miami International Airport, Tel: 305-876 7515. Key West International Airport is a small, regional airport that receives flights from Miami and other parts of the state, Tel: 305-296 5439. For departing international flights at all airports, check-in time is 90 min-

Miami is the largest cruise port in the world

utes prior to take-off. For domestic flights it's one hour.

By Rail

Amtrak, a passenger train service, brings travelers from around the country, Tel: (1-800) USA-RAIL. Its major stops in Florida include Tallahassee, Jacksonville, Orlando, Tampa, St Petersburg and Miami. While not in fact much cheaper than flying, Amtrak offers a glimpse of the countryside on comfortable trains that are equipped with sleeping bunks and dining-cars.

By Road

Although the state highway system of Florida makes for a rather boring drive, it's efficient, safe and well-maintained. Gas stations and rest stops are conveniently located, and road signs are easy to follow. The main north/south routes are I-75, I-95, and the Florida Turnpike which is a toll road. Coming from the west, the main route is I-10. Excellent road maps can be obtained for free by writing to the Florida Department of Commerce, Collins Building, Tallahassee, FL 32303.

The two main bus companies serving Florida from other parts of the country are Greyhound and Trailways. Bus stops are located in all major cities along with about 40 smaller ones. Although the service is adequate, many of the bus stops are located in neighborhoods where crime is a problem and caution is advised. Regional phone numbers are listed in local telephone directories.

TRAVEL ESSENTIALS

Visas and Customs

Visa and passport requirements vary with the country of origin and should be obtained through the relevant consulate. Foreigners visiting Florida are required to declare all items brought into the state to US Customs at the time of arrival. There is no limit on the amount of money or traveler's checks a visitor can bring into or take out of the US, but any amount over US $5,000 must be reported to US Customs. The duty-free allowance

for bringing goods into or out of the United States is 1 litre of liquor and 1 carton of cigarettes.

When to Visit

Winter is without doubt the best time to visit Florida. Americans and Europeans, fleeing the cold, venture into the state in record numbers. Hotel rates are therefore highest in winter, and reservations are essential. Summer months, although very hot, are also popular especially with American families and South Americans. The 'off season' – spring and fall months – is least crowded and least expensive.

Beach weather prevails

Weather

From the northernmost border to the southernmost tip, Florida has a moderate range of temperatures. Clear, sunny skies prevail year-round except for the summer months when afternoon thunderstorms and lightning strikes are common. More people are killed by lightning in Florida than in any other state. If you see lightning, the best advice is to head indoors; if you're driving in a car, stay in it. The humidity rate is generally high, and in summer months it soars – be prepared for a mild steam bath.

Hurricanes, as South Florida was recently reminded, do happen. Florida's hurricane season – the times when a storm is most likely to strike – is June through October. Coastal areas are at most risk but inland areas are also vulnerable. The National Weather Service, headquartered in Miami, carefully tracks all possible threats and alerts local communities of any impending danger. Evacuation routes and shelters are available if the threat becomes a reality.

Average Temperatures

Months	North	Central	South
Dec–Feb	44–68°F	50–72°F	60–76°F
March–May	62–84°F	66–85°F	70–85°F
June–Aug	71–88°F	73–92°F	75–93°F
Sept–Nov	52–72°F	60–76°F	67–84°F

Time Zones

All of Florida operates on Eastern Standard Time except for a small northwest section of the state that runs on Central Standard Time – an hour earlier. During Daylight Savings Time – from the last Sunday in April through the last Sunday in October – clocks are set 1 hour ahead.

What to Wear

When it comes to clothing, casual is the preferred style in Florida. A few upmarket restaurants require a jacket and tie for men during dinner, but most establishments encourage guests to dress as they please. Shorts, T-shirts and sneakers are acceptable for both men and women, but bathing suits should be reserved for the beach or swimming-pools only. In general, lightweight cotton clothing is the most practical. Bringing along a jacket or sweater is a good idea even in summer when air-conditioned restaurants can be as cold as Canada.

Electricity

Standard electrical sockets operate on a 110-VOLT current with 220-VOLT razor sockets available at most hotels. Electrical adapters can be purchased at many drugstores, or sometimes borrowed from a hotel concierge.

GETTING ACQUAINTED

Geography and Culture

As the southeastern peninsula of the US, Florida has a land area of over 58,000 sq miles – larger than England, Portugal or Greece. It's about 450 miles long and 150 miles wide with over 7,000 lakes, 34 rivers, and 1,000 miles of glorious beaches. Along the east coast lies the Atlantic Ocean, and to the west, the Gulf of Mexico. Its southernmost point is just 1,700 miles north of the equator.

Most of the state is flat, flat, flat. But in parts of central and northern Florida there are hills, although not very big ones. Oak, pine and cypress trees cover much of the rural land, and south of the Palm Beach County line palm trees and tropical plants are abundant.

A few Florida facts: Florida's nickname, the 'Sunshine State', was designated by the state's legislature in 1970; the state flower is the orange blossom; the state bird is the mockingbird; the state capital is Tallahassee; and the state song is *Old Folks at Home*, commonly known as *Suwannee River*.

With a fast-growing population of over 13 million, Florida no longer fits the *Old Folks At Home* image. Its reputation as a retirement haven is fading, and a recent influx of youthful immigrants and families from around the country has made Florida a booming sun-belt state. Its ethnic blend includes Native Americans, Hispanics, Jews, West Indians, African-

A portrait in Little Haiti

Americans, Yankees (Northerners), and Crackers (old-time Floridians whose ancestors sided with the South during the American Civil War). Although a predominantly Christian state, denominations of all the world's religions can be found along with quite a fair share of New Age sects.

MONEY MATTERS

Cash/Traveler's Checks/Credit Cards

All of Florida's international airports have exchange bureaus for converting foreign money. Banks will also exchange currencies. Banking hours are usually Monday to Friday 9am–3pm, but some are open on Saturday mornings too. Traveler's checks are accepted at most establishments as are major credit cards.

Automatic teller machines that dispense cash 24 hours a day are located in most airports, shopping centers and hotels. Systems available are Cirrus, Plus, MasterCard, Visa, Carte Blanche, Diners Club and American Express. American Express also has Express Cash which allows card-holders to withdraw up to US $2,500 from their personal checking accounts. The toll-free numbers for lost or stolen cards or traveler's checks are: for **Visa** 800-336 8472, **Mastercard** 800-800 4000, **American Express** 800-441 0519. Phone numbers for others are listed in local directories.

Taxes

Florida's state sales tax is 6 percent, but several counties add on their own tax, bringing the overall sales tax in some areas to 7 percent. There's also a bed tax levied, which varies from county to county, that adds another few percent to a hotel room rate.

Tipping

Gratuities are rarely included on restaurant bills, but if they are a notation will alert you of it. Otherwise, the standard tipping rate is somewhere between 15 and 20 percent depending on the quality of the service you receive. Tips for luggage handlers at airports or hotels are usually $1 per bag.

HOURS & HOLIDAYS

Business Hours

Most shops and offices are open Monday to Friday 9am–5pm with no closing hours for lunch. Most large shopping centers are open Monday-Saturday 10am–9.30pm and Sunday 10am–6pm.

Public Holidays

Banks and most businesses are closed during the following public holidays:

January 1:	New Year's Day
January 15:	Martin Luther King Day
3rd Monday in February:	Presidents Day
Last Monday in May:	Memorial Day
July 4:	Independence Day
1st Monday in September:	Labor Day
2nd Monday in October:	Columbus Day
November 11:	Veterans Day
4th Thursday in November:	Thanksgiving
December 25:	Christmas Day

Getting around is best by car

GETTING AROUND

Car

Unfortunately, it's difficult to get around in Florida without a car. Many of the larger hotels offer shuttle services to transport their guests to nearby attractions, but in order to explore on your own you must have transportation. If you're not driving into the state with your own car, it's a good idea to rent one. Valid driver's licences from other countries are accepted.

Rental car rates in Florida are relatively low and vary between companies. Rates are available per day, week or month and, depending on the season, the price for a small car can range from $75 to $150 per week. Most rental companies don't charge a mileage fee on top of this. Available vehicles include: economical compacts, luxury sedans, vans, motorcycles, motor-homes, campers, and convertibles. A few reliable companies are:

Avis	Tel: (1-800) 331 1212
Budget	Tel: (1-800) 527 0700
Dollar	Tel: (1-800) 307 7309
Hertz	Tel: (1-800) 654 3131
National	Tel: (1-800) 328 4567
Thrifty	Tel: (1-800) 367 2277

Driving Regulations

Speed limits on the highways are either 55 or 65mph depending on the municipality and road conditions. On the smaller roads the speed limit is between 20 and 40mph. Road signs indicate the local limits, which are strictly enforced by local police. Florida law allows drivers to make a right turn at a red light after the vehicle has come to a complete stop. Other state laws include: all traffic – on both sides of the street unless it is a divided highway – must stop while a school bus is loading or unloading children; passing is allowed in the left lane only; motorcyclists must wear helmets; and drivers and front-seat passengers must wear seat-belts.

Public Transportation

Public buses are available in most cites and hotel employees should be able to provide schedules and route information. Although inexpensive, they can be time-consuming and impractical. Tampa and Miami both have public, Metromover train systems convenient for sightseeing.

Taxis are available in most cities, but they aren't easy to hail from a street corner. Usually, a phone call in advance is needed for a pick-up. Rates average about $1.25 per mile no matter how many passenger share the car. An additional $1 charge is usually added to airport fares.

ACCOMMODATION

Accommodation in Florida ranges from modern, self-contained resorts to historic inns, youth hostels, and mom-and-pop motels. For general information on where to go contact the Florida Hotel/Motel Association, 200 West College Avenue, Tallahassee, FL 32301; Tel: 850-224 2888. Rates in the following list are for the lowest prices available per night for two people in the winter season: $ = under $75, $$ = $75–150, $$$ = $150–225, $$$$ = over $225. Rates on a weekly basis, and during the slow season, are less expensive.

Orlando Area

WYNDHAM PALACE RESORT
1900 Buena Vista Drive, Lake Buena Vista, FL 32380
Tel: 407-827 2727
One of Disney World's 'official' hotels, Wyndham Palace is a sprawling property with over 1,000 rooms, three pools, three tennis courts, a health club and several fine restaurants. A modern and well-managed resort. *$$*

KNIGHTS'S INN ORLANDO MAINGATE WEST
7475 West Irlo Bronson Highway, Kissimmee, FL 32746
Tel: 407-396 4200
A comfortable budget motel with a pool and non-smoker rooms. *$*

COURTYARD AT LAKE LUCERNE
211 North Lucerne Circle East, Orlando, FL 32801
Tel: 407-648 5188
One of the finest inns in the state featuring Victorian antiques, hearty breakfasts, and down-home hospitality. *$$*

The Metromover, Miami

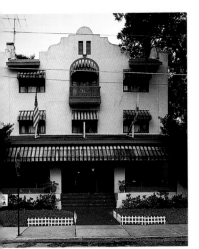

The Orlando Youth Hostel

ORLANDO INTERNATIONAL YOUTH HOSTEL
227 North Eola Drive, Orlando, FL 32801
Tel: 407-843 8888
The best bargain in Orlando, this hostel sits beside a beautiful park in downtown Orlando. It has 90 dormitory-style beds that cost less than $15 per night. Also runs special flat-rate (75¢) bus to Orlando's main attractions. $

THE PEABODY
9801 International Drive,
Orlando, FL 32819
Tel: 407-352 4000
High-rise, first-class hotel which caters to adults and children. The hotel's theme is ducks, and every morning a parade of mallards struts through the lobby. $$$

Tampa/St Petersburg Area

HYATT REGENCY DOWNTOWN
211 North Tampa Street,
Tampa, FL 33602
Tel: 813-225 1234
Sophisticated downtown hotel in the business district. Within easy walking distance of shopping and museums. $$

BAYBORO HOUSE
1719 Beach Drive SE,
St Petersburg, FL 33701
Tel: 727-823 4955
An old, gable-roofed inn with rocking chairs on the front porch. Located across the street from Tampa Bay. Quiet, cozy and warm. $

THE HERITAGE
234 3rd Avenue North,
St Petersburg, FL 33701
Tel: 727-822 4814
A calming bed-and-breakfast inn dedicated to historic preservation in the heart of downtown. A small pool and popular restaurant. $$

HOLIDAY INN BUSCH GARDENS
2701 East Fowler Avenue,
Tampa, FL 33612
Tel: 813-971 4710
A family-oriented motel with a pool, exercise room and restaurant just a mile from Busch Gardens. $$

Miami Area

CORDOZO
1300 Ocean Drive,
Miami Beach, FL 33139
Tel: 305-535 6500
An oceanfront, Art Deco sweetheart of a hotel in the historic Art Deco District. Nice rooms and good service. $$

FONTAINEBLEAU HILTON
4441 Collins Avenue,
Miami Beach, FL 33140
Tel: 305-538 2000

The Hyatt Regency, Tampa

One of the grand-style hotels from the 1950s with over 1,000 rooms, ocean views, health spa, and a waterfall swimming-pool. $$$

HYATT REGENCY MIAMI
400 SE 2nd Avenue, Miami, FL 33131
Tel: 305-358 1234
A modern, business district hotel within walking distance of downtown shopping. $$

MAYFAIR HOUSE
3000 Florida Avenue, Miami, FL 33133
Tel: 305-441 0000
In the center of Coconut Grove, the Mayfair is an architectural gem with luxurious rooms and first-class restaurants. $$$$

MIAMI RIVER INN
118 SW South River Drive,
Miami, FL 33130
Tel: 305-325 0045
A charming hotel with old-time Florida style set beside the Miami river in Little Havana. $$

Key West

OCEAN KEY HOUSE
Zero Duval Street, Key West, FL 33040
Tel: 305-296 7701
A plush, all-suite hotel with water views and jacuzzis in all rooms. Perfect for catching a Key West sunset and cruising through town. $$$$

PIER HOUSE
1 Duval Street, Key West, FL 33040
Tel: 305-296 4600
With the feel of a secluded island, the Pier House is a luxury resort with a private beach and beautiful rooms. At the foot of downtown's main street. $$$$

THE CURRY MANSION
511 Caroline Street, Key West, FL 33040
Tel: 305-294 5349
A tropical-style Victorian mansion reborn as a bed-and-breakfast inn. Owners Al and Edith Amsterdam always make their guests feel welcome. $$$

ISLAND CITY HOUSE
422 William Street, Key West, FL 33040
Tel: 305-294 5702
Off the main strip, this tropical garden hotel is a soothing oasis with comfortable rooms. $$$

SOUTHERNMOST MOTEL
1319 Duval Street, Key West, FL 33040
Tel: 305-294 5539
A quaint motel with a beautiful pool and full-service concierge. $$

HEALTH & EMERGENCIES
Medical and Dental Services

Most cities in Florida have walk-in medical and dental clinics that require no affiliation or insurance (payment is due upon treatment). For severe medical emergencies that require immediate attention, calling the local emergency phone number will dispatch an ambulance at any time of day or night. The toll-free, three-digit number is the same throughout the state: **911**.

The following hospitals offer 24-hour emergency room care: Orlando Regional Medical Center, 9400 Turkey Lake Road, Orlando, Tel: 407-351 8500; University Community Hospital, 3100 East Fletcher Avenue, Tampa, Tel: 813-971 6000; Jackson Memorial Medical Center, 1611 NW 12th Avenue, Miami, Tel: 305-585 1111; Florida Keys Memorial Hospital, 5900 Junior College Road, Key West, Tel: 305-294 5531.

Pharmacies

Most pharmacies are open daily 9am–9pm. The following are open 24 hours: Eckerd Drugs, 670 Lee Road, Orlando, Tel: 407-644-6908; Eckerd Drugs, 8925 Terrace Road, Tampa, Tel: 813-988 5214; Walgreens, 5731 Bird Road, Miami, Tel: 305-666 0757.

Poolside at the Pier House

Mail boxes in Key West

Crime

To reach the police in an emergency wherever you are in the state dial 911. Non-emergency numbers vary according to the city and can be found in the local telephone directory.

Crime is a nuisance that tourism officials wish would go away, but unfortunately it's here to stay. Although, when compared to urban areas in other parts of the country, the crime rate in Florida is relatively low, it does pose a possible problem for travelers. Criminals can easily spot tourists – cameras, sunburned faces, foreign accents, wallets full of money and Mickey Mouse T-shirts are clear markings. The best advice is to deposit extra cash and jewelry in hotel safes, never leave luggage unattended, and keep a close eye on purses and shoulder bags.

The most recent trend in tourist crime targets the drivers of rental cars. Since most rental cars are marked as such, they too attract the attention of criminals. If driving alone, never leave a bag on the passenger seat – robbers have been known to throw rocks through windows while cars are stopped at traffic lights. For added protection, store all valuables in the trunk while driving or parked.

Although caution is advised, don't let the fear of crime dampen a vacation. Florida's cities – including Miami – are not as dangerous as their reputation portrays them. Talking to locals is still a safe, and enjoyable, thing to do.

COMMUNICATIONS & NEWS

Post

Post office hours vary, but in general they are open Monday to Friday 9am–5pm, and on Saturday 9am–noon. Tourists can have mail delivered to most main post offices by having it sent to their name in care of General Delivery. Postage stamps are sold at post offices and at most hotels, pharmacies, airports and supermarkets. Overnight delivery services and package deliveries are available through the US Post Office, United Parcel Service, and Federal Express.

Telephone

Public telephones are located at hotels, gas stations, restaurants, shopping centers and most public places. The toll is 25¢ or 35¢ at all phones in the state. Long-distance calls are the least expensive on weekends and after 5pm on weekdays. The five main area codes in Florida are 813, 904, 407, 850 and 305. Numbers with an 800 area code are toll-free. For calls outside the local area codes dial 1 + the area code + the number. For operator assistance dial 0.

To dial other countries, first dial the international access code 011, then the country code: Australia (61); France (33); Germany (49); Italy (39); Japan (81); Mexico (52); Spain (34); United Kingdom (44). If using a US phone credit card, dial the company's access number below, then 01, then the country code. Sprint, Tel: 1010333; AT&T, Tel: 1010288.

Media

There are over 100 newspapers across the state. The award-winning *Miami Herald* is the most comprehensive paper in Florida, and the *Orlando Sentinel*, *St Petersburg Times*, and *Tampa Tribune* are also good news sources. Out-of-state and foreign papers can be bought at most newsstands and hotel gift shops. All major Florida cities have television stations affiliated with the major national networks, and many hotels offer free cable television with a wide choice of channels.

SPORTS

Fishing

Florida's coastline is an angler's dream with over 600 varieties of fish including marlin, kingfish, sailfish, dolphin, sea trout and shark. Whether it's deep-sea fishing by boat or surf-casting from shore,

An angler's dream

Florida salt-water fishing is good year-round. The fresh-water fishing is also good in the state's many lakes, rivers and streams, and in the Florida Everglades. Licences are required for fresh-water fishing; for information call the Florida Game and Fresh Water Fish Commission, Tel: 850-488 3641. Salt-water fishing requires no licence; for information on fishing areas call the Florida Department of Natural Resources, Tel: 850-488 7326. If you forget to pack your rod and reel, there are many shops that rent fishing equipment by the day.

Tennis and Golf

With over 7,700 clay, grass and hard tennis courts, it's no wonder that Florida has become a major sponsor of international matches. The Florida Tennis Association, Tel: 954-968 3434, can point you in the direction of the nearest public or private court. And when it comes to golf, Florida beats all other states. For information on the over 1,000 public and private courses, contact the Florida Sports Foundation, Tel: 850-488 8347.

Jai-Alai

Jai-Alai, the word's fastest sport, made its way to Florida from the Basque area of Spain and now has a substantial audience. The game, similar to hand-ball, is played in courts called frontons, and betting is a part of the fun. For information on one of the eight frontons in Florida call the Department of Business Regulations, Tel: 850-470 5675.

Horse/Dog Racing

For those who feel lucky at the track, Florida has thoroughbred horse-racing, harness-racing, and greyhound-racing. For information on tracks, schedules, and betting practices, call the Department of Business Regulations, Tel: 850-470 5675.

Other Sports

Scuba Diving: For information throughout the state call the Florida Association of Dive Operators, Tel: 850-222 6000.
Professional Football: Miami Dolphins, Tel: 305-620 2578; Tampa Bay Buccaneers, Tel: 813-879 2827.

Professional Basketball: Miami Heat, Tel: 954-835 7000; Orlando Magic, Tel: 407-896 2442.
Professional Baseball: Florida Marlins, Tel: 305-626 7400.

USEFUL ADDRESSES

Tourist Offices

The main office for the state's tourism authority Visit Florida is at 126 West Van Buren Street, Tallahassee, FL 32399; Tel: 850-488 5607. If you telephone or write to this office in advance of your visit to Florida, staff will forward information packs. The following are regional offices:

Orlando/Orange County Convention & Visitor's Bureau, 7208 Sand Lake Road, suite 300, Orlando, FL 32819.
Tel: 407-363 5872.

Kissimmee/St Cloud Convention & Visitor's Bureau, 1925 Irlo Bronson Memorial Highway, Kissimmee, FL 34742.
Tel: 407-847 5000.

Florida's Space Coast Office of Tourism, 2725 St John's Street, Melbourne, FL 32940.
Tel: 321-633 2110.

Tampa/Hillsborough Convention & Visitor's Bureau, 111 Madison Street, Tampa, FL 33602.
Tel: 813-223 1111.

St Petersburg Area Chamber of Commerce, PO Box 1371, St Petersburg, FL 33731. Tel: 727-821 4069.

Greater Miami Convention & Visitor's Bureau, 701 Brickell Avenue, Miami, FL 33132.
Tel: 305-539 3000.

Consulates

All of the following consulate offices are in Miami:

Denmark: Tel: 305-446 0020
Germany: Tel: 305-358 0290
United Kingdom: Tel: 305-374 1522

Italy: Tel: 305-374 6322
Japan: Tel: 305-530 9090

FURTHER READING

The Florida Keys – a History and Guide by Joy Williams, Random House, New York, 1987.

Guide to the Small and Historic Lodgings of Florida by Herbert Hiller, Pineapple Press, Sarasota, 1988.

Insight Compact Guide: Florida Keys edited by Joann Biondi, Apa Publications, Singapore, 1993.

Insight Guide: Florida edited by Paul Zach, Apa Publications, Singapore, 1998. Comprehensive coverage plus features on treasure-hunting, food, space exploration, etc.

Insight Pocket Guide: Miami edited by Joann Biondi, Apa Publications, Singapore, 1998.

Time to refresh

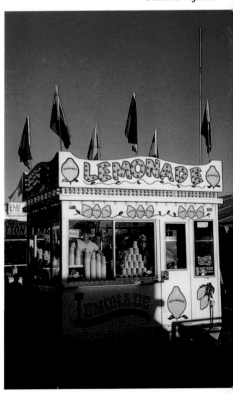

Index

Acknowledgments

Photography	**Tony Arruza** *and*
Front cover	**Paul Rees/Tony Stone Images**
Back cover	**NASA**
Pages 39T, 43	**Busch Gardens**
24B, 25, 26T, 26B, 27	**© Disney**
12T	**Henry Morrison Fagler Museum**
15	**Ricardo Ferro**
12B	**Florida Division of Tourism**
5B, 77	**Catherine Karnow**
14, 23T, 28, 30, 31T, 31B, 44, 57, 60, 65, 70B, 72T, 81, 89	**Bud Lee**
16B	**Universal Studios**
33	**Paul Zach**
Handwriting	**V Barl**
Cover Design	**Tanvir Virdee**
Cartography	**Berndtson & Berndtson**

NOTES

INSIGHT
Pocket Guides

Insight Pocket Guides pioneered a new approach to guidebooks, introducing the concept of the authors as "local hosts" who would provide readers with personal recommendations, just as they would give honest advice to a friend who came to stay. They also included a full-size pull-out map.

Now, to cope with the needs of the 21st century, new editions in this growing series are being given a new look to make them more practical to use, and restaurant and hotel listings have been greatly expanded.

Also from Insight Guides...

Insight Guides is the classic series, providing the complete picture with expert and informative text and stunning photography. Each book is an ideal travel planner, a reliable on-the-spot companion - and a superb visual souvenir of a trip. 193 titles.

Insight Maps are designed to complement the guidebooks. They provide full mapping of major destinations, and their laminated finish gives them ease of use and durability. 65 titles.

Insight Compact Guides are handy reference books, modestly priced yet comprehensive. The text, pictures and maps are all cross-referenced, making them ideal books to consult while seeing the sights. 119 titles.

INSIGHT POCKET GUIDE TITLES